ELVIS!

ELVIS!

Richard Wootton

RANDOM HOUSE 🏠 NEW YORK

First American edition, 1985.
Copyright © 1982 by Richard Wootton. All rights reserved under International and Pan-American Copyright Conventions. Published in the United States by Random House, Inc., New York. Originally published in Great Britain as ELVIS PRESLEY in 1982 by Hodder and Stoughton Ltd.

Library of Congress Cataloging in Publication Data: Wootton, Richard. Elvis! Reprint. Originally published: London : Hodder and Stoughton, 1982 (1984 printing). Includes index. SUMMARY: A biography of one of the most popular record artists of all time. 1. Presley, Elvis, 1935–1977—Juvenile literature. 2. Singers—United States—Biography—Juvenile literature. 3. Rock musicians—United States—Biography—Juvenile literature. [1. Presley, Elvis, 1935–1977. 2. Singers] I. Title ML3930.P73W66 1985 784.5'4'00924 [B] [92] 84-17970
ISBN: 0-394-87046-8 (trade); 0-394-97046-2 (lib. bdg.)

The publishers have made every effort to locate the owners of all copyrighted material and photographs and to obtain permission to reprint photographs and quoted passages in this book. Any errors are unintentional, and corrections will be made in future editions if necessary.

Photo credits: Jacques Delessert: 17, 54 bottom, 107, 120; Elvis Presley Fan Club: 9, 33, 59, 63 top, 71 bottom, 77, 85, 89, 90, 96, 105, 112, 121 bottom; Martin Hawkins: 23, 28, 46; Stephen Holland: 19, 30, 37, 38, 53, 71 top; Melody Maker: 121 top; RCA Records: 13, 40, 43, 63 bottom, 66, 87, 93, 99; Syndication International: 74; Tennessee Department of Tourist Development: 54 top, 116.

Manufactured in the United States of America
1 2 3 4 5 6 7 8 9 0

Contents

For Judith
with love and thanks

1

Childhood

Elvis Aaron Presley was born early in the morning of January 8, 1935. He was one of a pair of identical twins, but his brother, who had the matching name of Jesse Garon Presley, was still-born and was buried the next day in a small, unmarked grave at the local cemetery.

Elvis's parents, Vernon and Gladys Presley, were extremely poor. They came from farming families and lived in Tupelo, a small town in northeast Mississippi.

They grew up in homes just a few streets from each other. Neither Gladys nor Vernon spent more than a few years at school, and they had no special skills. They married in 1933, when he was seventeen and she was twenty-one.

America was in the midst of the Great Depression. It was a time when millions of people were unemployed. Many more were badly paid and struggled to earn enough money to pay for food and a roof over their heads.

Vernon never had a job that lasted for more than a few months. He took work where he could find it, most often as a farm laborer, and though he worked long hours, the pay was low. Gladys had a job as a sewing machine operator at the Tupelo Garment Company.

They lived in the poorest part of the town, near the railroad tracks, in a humble two-room wooden shack that Vernon had built with his father. The house was raised a few inches from the ground on wooden stilts because the ground was often flooded when nearby creeks overflowed their banks.

The little house was typical of thousands of poor people's homes in the days of the Depression. They were sometimes called "shotgun shacks." Some people say this was because they were like the two barrels of a shotgun; others, that it was because you could stand at the front door and shoot a shotgun out of the back door.

There were two square rooms: a bedroom at the front, a kitchen at the back. There was no bathroom, and water had to be fetched from a nearby pump.

The family was poorer than ever when Elvis arrived. Gladys had given up her job, and Vernon was delivering milk—another low-paying job. So Elvis Presley, who would one day earn more money than any other entertainer in the world, was born into a family that struggled constantly to pay for the most basic necessities of life.

Medical treatment cost money, so poor people like the Presleys couldn't afford to have their babies in a hospital. There was a doctor present at their home for the birth, but he didn't realize that Gladys was going to have twins until after Elvis was born and she was still in pain.

No one knows if little Jesse Garon would have survived if Gladys had been in a hospital, but Elvis would later say, "My little brother died, and my mama almost died, because we couldn't afford to go to a hospital." Later, when he became rich and famous, Elvis frequently traveled with a personal physician and was very generous in giving to charities that paid for medical treatment for the children of poor families.

The Presleys were very proud of their little boy. Though they had very little money, they scrimped and saved to make him happy and healthy. Any spare cash would go toward "something for Elvis." They impressed on him that though he came from poor folks, he was as good as anyone else in the world.

They instilled in Elvis a strong feeling of self-respect, and he always seems to have known he was important and destined for something special. But they also taught him to be very polite and respectful of others. He was very fond of his mother, and when he was a young man would call her "my best girl."

The "shotgun shack" where Elvis was born in 1935.

No one has ever described Elvis as a particularly normal little boy, and he certainly didn't have a normal childhood. He was very quiet and shy and had few friends. Gladys pampered him and didn't like it whenever he left her, even to go off to play with other children.

"My mama never let me out of her sight," Elvis recalled in an interview years later. "I couldn't go down to the creek like all the other kids. Sometimes when I was little, I used to run off. Mama would whip me, and I thought she didn't love me."

But Gladys was cross because she had a great fear of losing her son. She used to dream about him every night, and frequently she awoke from nightmares in which something awful had happened to him. She had been told by a doctor that she couldn't have any more children, so she devoted herself to looking after Elvis. Having already lost Jesse, she was determined that nothing should happen to her remaining little boy.

Mr. and Mrs. Presley were regular churchgoers, and they took Elvis with them whenever they visited the First Assembly of God Church on Adams Street, Tupelo, which was a few blocks from their house.

Both of them were pleased when their boy showed an early interest in gospel singing. By the time he was two years old, Elvis was trying to sing, and though he couldn't manage the words, he could carry the tune and swayed with the rhythm.

"We were a religious family," said Elvis later, "going around together to sing at camp meetings and revivals. Since I was two years old, all I knew was gospel music. That music became such a part of my life, it was as natural as dancing. A way to escape from the problems, and my way of release."

The Presleys' local Pentecostal church was not one of

those where the congregation sat quietly and solemnly through a service. People would rock back and forth in their pews, sometimes falling to the floor and shouting out things like "Praise the Lord" and "Thank you, God." The preachers were the most lively, calling out, sometimes "speaking in tongues" (a form of prayer in which the speech is impossible to understand), and being very un-inhibited in their movements.

Elvis's most vivid memories of his early childhood were of going to church, and he was convinced that both the music and the behavior of the preachers influenced his own singing and the way he performed—including his controversial stage movements, which caused a sensation after television and concert appearances in 1956.

"During the singing," Elvis recalled, "the preachers used to cut up all over the place—that's how I was in-troduced to the onstage wiggle. The preachers did it. And the congregation loved it—why, I even remember one day a preacher jumping on a piano. I liked them, and I guess I learned a lot from them."

Elvis loved singing at church, and when he was old enough he went to the Wednesday revival meetings to learn religious spirituals. He never had singing lessons, so it was the nearest he came to any kind of proper music training.

His parents knew he had a talent for singing, but it wasn't recognized at school until he was eight years old, and then only for a brief period.

Most schools have one or two pupils like Elvis, children who are very quiet, well behaved, and don't shine at any-thing in particular. They go through their school career without making any significant impression on the other children or the teachers.

Elvis was like this, except for one day at the East Tupelo

Consolidated School, when a teacher named Mrs. Grimes heard Elvis sing a sad song about a boy and his dog. She was very touched by the performance and asked the principal, Mr. Cole, to listen.

He liked what he heard, too, and took the small eight-year-old boy to the annual Mississippi-Alabama Agricultural Fair and entered him in the children's talent competition.

Elvis had to climb onto a wooden chair to reach the microphone, and he sang "Old Shep," the same song that had impressed his teachers. He won second prize, which was five dollars and as many rides on the amusements as he wanted.

This event seems to have been the only time in Elvis's childhood when he gave any hint that he might one day become a performer. When he became famous, years later, the teachers and former pupils at the school couldn't recall anything else about him.

It was soon after the talent show that the Presleys were so down on their luck that they had to move from their home. Vernon wasn't making enough money to keep up the payments on their little house, even though he was often working twelve hours a day. They moved in with some relatives.

Vernon had a brother named Vester (who had married Gladys's sister Cletis), and he owned a battered old guitar, which he didn't really know how to play. When Elvis showed an interest in the instrument, Vester taught him the few chords he knew.

One day Elvis asked his parents if he could have a bicycle for his birthday. Sadly they had to explain to him that bicycles were far too expensive, but perhaps he would like a guitar like his uncle Vester's.

"I really wanted that bicycle," Elvis remembered, "but

Daddy couldn't afford one. So he bought me a guitar for around twelve bucks. I know even this was a great sacrifice—he went without smokes for several weeks."

Elvis loved that guitar and taught himself to play by listening to records and copying the music he heard on the radio. People didn't have television in those days, and the radio was the main source of entertainment.

He liked the music shows best and listened to all kinds. His favorites were the religious gospel music programs of people like Sister Rosetta Tharpe, the hillbilly (now called country) music by singers like Roy Acuff, Ernest Tubb, and Jimmie Rodgers, and the blues played by black musicians like Arthur "Big Boy" Crudup and Muddy Waters.

A family of the Great Depression: Gladys and Vernon Presley with Elvis, age 2.

Elvis's parents scolded him when he listened to blues, because they considered it "sinful" and "dirty" music, so he had to listen in secret. They associated blues with drinking alcohol, gambling, immorality, and the low-life clubs where it was usually played—places where church-goers should never be found.

Blues was also the music of black people, and at that time in the South, white people did not normally mix with blacks. Those were the days of segregation, when buses had "whites only" and "black" areas, when white and black people lived separate lives, shopped at different stores, went to different schools, and listened to different radio stations.

But Mississippi had a higher proportion of black people than any other state in the country, and it was inevitable that poor white people, like the Presleys, would live close to poor blacks and share similar experiences and cultural backgrounds. Elvis's home was very near the Tupelo black ghetto called Shakerag, and he would later recall hearing black men playing guitars and singing country blues on their front porches.

Elvis found black music exciting, particularly the records he heard on the radio, with the powerful sound of the electric guitars and the strong pounding beat of the drums.

2

Memphis,
Tennessee

As Elvis grew older, Vernon Presley was finding it increasingly difficult to get regular work. In 1948, when his son was thirteen, Vernon reluctantly decided that the family would have to move to the big city of Memphis, Tennessee (which was about one hundred miles northwest of Tupelo). There, he was sure, things could only get better.

Elvis later recalled the move: "We were broke, man, broke, and we left Tupelo overnight. Dad packed all our belongings in boxes and put them on the top and in the trunk of a 1939 Plymouth. We just headed for Memphis."

At first the Presleys' living conditions in Memphis were worse than they'd ever been. The only home they could afford was a cramped single room in a house on Poplar Avenue. There were no cooking facilities, and the bathroom had to be shared with several other poor families.

Poplar Avenue was in the downtown area of Memphis.

As in many other cities at the time, the downtown was the poorest part. When the houses were first built on Poplar Avenue, they were lived in by wealthy families, but as the buildings grew older and the area became more crowded, those people moved to the outskirts of town and newer, bigger houses. The street, like the rest of the downtown area, became increasingly run-down, and the houses were split into apartments or single-room dwellings.

In 1948, the Presley home at 572 Poplar Avenue was a horrible place to live. The family had to do everything in one room; the heating was inadequate; the electrical wiring was dangerous.

Elvis was certainly unhappy when they first moved in. His cousins and few friends were all back in Tupelo, and now he had to go to a new school, L. C. Humes High on Manassas Avenue, a huge, drab building which housed 1,700 teenagers.

On the first day, Vernon took Elvis to school and then went home. Back at Poplar Avenue he discovered his son, who had run home, terrified of the building and all the unfamiliar faces.

The next day Elvis was back and gradually got used to the size of the place, though he never seems to have had many friends. His mother was still very protective—several people apparently told her she was "overprotective"; but it didn't stop her from walking him to school, although he was now a teenager and should have been capable of looking after himself.

Vernon found a steady job as a paint packer at the United Paint factory, Gladys worked as a nurses' aide at St. Joseph's Hospital, and Elvis mowed lawns after school, giving nearly all the money to his parents. They, in turn, gave him any money he needed.

Things improved slightly. The family moved to a two-

Left: *L. C. Humes High, now a junior high school, which Elvis attended between 1948 and 1953.* Right: *Lauderdale Court, where the Presley family had a two-bedroom apartment.*

bedroom apartment in Lauderdale Court, part of a government housing project for low-income families, which was near their old house and still in the poorest part of Memphis.

They had a nicer home but other problems arose. Gladys was gaining weight and was frequently ill. She had to give up her job and the family had less money. So Elvis found a job in the evenings at Loews Palace, a cinema on Union Avenue.

He didn't work there long because another usher reported him to the manager for watching the movies rather than showing people to their seats. He was fired.

Elvis loved movies, though he hadn't seen any until he came to Memphis, and he was to enjoy them for the rest of his life. Once he was in a theater, he couldn't take his eyes off the screen, which is why he was so bad at the job at Loews.

He got another job working on the evening shift for a company that made metal products. But this work made

17

him tired in the daytime, and it wasn't unusual for him to fall asleep in class.

When his mother discovered that his school studies were suffering because of his extra work, she insisted that he give up the job, and she struggled back to work.

Only a few of the teachers and students at Humes High School can remember much about Elvis until his final months at the school. He liked football, but wasn't very good; did reasonably well at his work, but never stood out in any way. One ex-Humes student remembered: "He had no personality, if you know what I mean. Just acted kind of goofy, sitting in the back of the class, playing his guitar. No one knew he was going to be anything."

However, toward the end of his school career Elvis changed his appearance quite dramatically, and suddenly he stood out from the crowd. All the other boys had short crew cuts, but Elvis grew his hair long and had sideburns. He said later that he did it "because that's how truck drivers wore theirs." He wanted to be a truck driver, just like his father. "Dad mostly drove trucks, and when he used to bring them home, I used to sit in them."

Elvis's haircut got him into trouble with other boys. Red West, a pupil at Humes High who was later to become his personal assistant, remembers: "If he had a regular haircut like the rest of us, he probably wouldn't have been bothered. But I guess the other kids thought he was trying to show off or something. I have never known any other human being to take more time over his hair. He would spend hours on it, smoothing it and combing it."

The other boys teased him about his appearance and Red saved him from being bullied a couple of times. Red remembers coming into the school washroom once and finding Elvis surrounded by four or five boys.

"They were pushing him up against the wall, and grabbing him from behind. They decided they were going to cut his hair. When I saw Elvis's face, it just triggered off something inside me. There was that look of real fear on his face. I said, 'Now, if you cut his hair, you're gonna have to cut my hair too, and that's gonna develop into

Top: *Elvis with three of his friends in Memphis, probably in 1953.* Right: *Elvis wore his hair long and had sideburns because he wanted to look like a truck driver.*

something else.' " Red had a tough-guy reputation, and the boys let Elvis go.

Elvis wore outrageous clothes, which he bought from a shop called Lansky Brothers on Beale Street. They sold costumes to entertainers, and their windows were filled with bright, jazzy items like pink sports coats and yellow corduroy jackets fringed with leopard skin. Bernard Lansky remembers: "He was about seventeen or eighteen and he would come over and press his nose against the window, like it was a candy store."

To the frequent taunting and baiting from fellow students, Elvis began going to school in these clothes; a combination of pink and black was a particular favorite.

While visiting Beale Street, which was a mile from his home, near the Mississippi River, Elvis also listened to the black musicians who played in the clubs and on the streets.

Beale Street has a reputation as the "home of the blues." Black musicians came from the surrounding rural areas to the street to try and make money, perhaps earning enough to pay for a trip north to Chicago or one of the other big industrial cities where there was work and more money.

Music was becoming increasingly important to Elvis, and he spent hours playing the guitar and singing, though almost always in private. There seem to have been only two occasions during his school days when he performed in public.

Elvis was surprised when he found that a teacher had entered him in a school concert, because he didn't think anyone knew that he sang. He performed a song called "Cold, Cold Icy Fingers" and did so well that he had to come back at the end for an encore.

Red West remembers: "He was an easy winner. He

seemed to be amazed that for the first time in his life, someone, other than his family, really liked him. At last, it seemed, he had found a way to make outsiders love him. As shy as he was, he had a definite magic on stage. After the show he just seemed to go back to being ordinary old Elvis."

The other public appearance came when, as a member of the Odd Fellows Boys' Club, he sang and played guitar during a show put on for the patients at the Memphis Veterans Hospital.

Only in hindsight do these two events give any clue to his future career. No one guessed at the time that he was going to be a professional musician, including Elvis, whose principal ambition seemed to be a life as a truck driver.

Elvis left school in 1953, at a time when his parents were very down on their luck. They'd fallen behind with their rent and had been evicted from Lauderdale Court. Their new apartment, on Cypress Street, wasn't much better than the awful room on Poplar Avenue.

Vernon had hurt his back and missed a lot of work, and Gladys was still ill, though she struggled to work at the hospital during the day and mended other people's clothes at night. No one had any idea that in a few years their fortunes would change dramatically, though Elvis had a feeling that something would happen to him.

His first job after leaving school was at the Precision Tool Company. He didn't like it, and found another job driving a truck for the Crown Electric Company, at $45 a week. As he would later recall, "When I was driving my truck, and one of them big shiny cars went by, it started me to daydreaming. I always felt that someday, somehow, something would change for me. I don't know exactly what, but it was a feeling that the future looked kinda bright."

He was less self-conscious about his singing by this time and enjoyed performing for anyone who'd listen, including the local firemen who seemed to have plenty of time on their hands.

Driving around Memphis, making deliveries for Crown Electric, Elvis frequently passed an office on Union Avenue that advertised the Memphis Recording Service. It was part of the Sun record company, which was owned by a man named Sam Phillips, and it offered the chance for anyone to make one copy of a 10-inch record for $4.

One lunchtime in 1953, Elvis decided to make a record for his mother's birthday. Playing the guitar, which he took with him everywhere in the Ford pickup truck, he sang a country ballad, "That's When Your Heartaches Begin," and "My Happiness," which he knew as a song by the popular Ink Spots group. By his own reckoning it sounded like "someone banging a trash can lid," but the engineer, Marion Keisker (who worked as secretary, receptionist, and almost everything else at Sun) was sufficiently impressed that she taped part of the recording to play to her boss when he returned from lunch. He liked what he heard and told Marion to keep the young man's name and address.

Gladys Presley loved her special record. "She borrowed a record player from a neighbor and played it over and over again until it was plumb wore out," said Elvis.

Sam Phillips had been raised on a plantation and always liked the songs and singing of the black workers, who seemed to him much better at expressing power and emotion in music than white people. He'd recorded several fine bluesmen at the Sun studios, including Howlin' Wolf, B. B. King, and Bobby Bland, and sold the masters to famous blues labels in Chicago and on the West Coast. He'd also released some on his own Sun label.

The Sun Recording Studio in Memphis, as it looks today.

In the days of segregation, records by black musicians were sold almost exclusively to black people. The white record-buying market was far larger, and Sam knew that however good the blues records were, they couldn't be big sellers. He frequently told people, "If I could only find a white boy who could sing like a black man, I would make a lot of money."

Elvis Presley was to prove him right, but at that point Sam hadn't connected the young man with the battered guitar and the torn jeans with his idea.

Elvis had ambitions to sing in a gospel group. "I always wanted to be in a gospel quartet. When I was sixteen I went to the Ellis Auditorium in Memphis to an all-night

23

gospel session. I went alone because none of the kids of my age liked that kind of music."

Several times during lunch Elvis parked his truck near the WMPS radio station and went to watch the live broadcast of *High Noon Roundup*, hosted by Memphis disc jockey Bob Neal, which featured country music and gospel. Making friends with a member of the Songfellows (a junior division of the popular Blackwood Brothers Quartet), Elvis nearly got a job replacing someone who was leaving, but the singer changed his mind at the last minute and didn't go.

Meanwhile a card with his misspelled name, "Elvis Pessley," was kept on the Sun files. Several months after Elvis made the record for his mother, Sam Phillips was looking for a singer to perform a new song he'd come across, when he took up Marion Keisker's suggestion, "What about the singer with sideburns?"

It was three o'clock on a Saturday afternoon in the early summer of 1954 when Sam spoke to Elvis on the telephone and asked him if he could come right over. Presley ran the one and a half miles to the studio and arrived panting a few minutes later. The professional singing career of Elvis Presley was about to begin.

3

The
Sun Days

Sam Phillips's small studio was housed in a shabby-looking one-story building at 706 Union Avenue on one of the busiest and best known streets in the city. It was in the heart of downtown Memphis, the area where Elvis had spent most of his teenage years—close to Beale Street, the house on Poplar Avenue, the movie theater where he had had the short-lived job as an usher, and Humes High School.

There were three rooms: a reception area where Marion Keisker managed the business side of the company; the twelve-by-twelve-foot studio with soundproof boards on the walls and ceiling, a piano, stools, and a cluster of microphones; and Sam Phillips's control room, where he kept his recording equipment and supervised the musicians.

While Elvis recovered his breath after the run, Sam played a demonstration record he'd been sent of a song

25

called "Without You." He really liked it and would have released it on Sun, but he didn't know the singer's name or who owned the copyright. So he wanted Elvis to make a version of it.

Presley listened carefully a couple of times to memorize the words and the tune, then stood at the microphone with his battered guitar and sang. Everyone present agreed that the result sounded dreadful, so he tried again, but it was not much better. Sam realized that his ideas for the song wouldn't work with Elvis, so he asked Elvis what else he could sing.

"I can do anything, sir," Marion remembers Elvis replying, and then he demonstrated by singing a variety of songs that he'd learned from the radio and records: soft pop ballads, some country, a few religious songs, and several tunes by popular comedian and singer Dean Martin (who was one of his favorites).

Phillips thought that Elvis had real talent but needed to work with other musicians—until then he'd always played and sung on his own. He arranged for Elvis to meet two members of the Starlight Wranglers, a group that wanted to record for Sun: Scotty Moore, a guitarist, and Bill Black, who played upright bass.

The three began rehearsing some songs by well-known country singers of the day, including Hank Snow and Eddy Arnold. In early July 1954 they went into the studio to try and make some recordings. They practiced a few songs, then taped a slow, mournful tune called "I Love You Because."

Then they took a break. It was to be one of the most famous breaks in the history of popular music. According to Scotty Moore, who's probably been asked about it several thousand times, "We were having Cokes and coffees, and all of a sudden Elvis started singing a song, jumping around and acting the fool, and then Bill picked up his bass and started acting the fool too, and then I started playing. Sam, I think, had the door to the control booth open—I don't know, he was either editing some tapes or doing something—and he stuck his head out and said, 'What are you doing?' And we said, 'We don't know.' 'Well back up,' he says. 'Try to find a place to start and do it again!' "

The recording they made then was of a blues song called "That's All Right" by one of Elvis's favorite musicians, Arthur "Big Boy" Crudup. But it didn't come out sounding like a blues tune. Elvis wasn't trying to copy the original version but sang in an unusual style, high and breathless, while Scotty and Bill sounded like country musicians playing at double or triple speed.

At another session, a day or two later, Elvis was again fooling around, this time with one of his favorite country songs, "Blue Moon of Kentucky." It was another unusual-sounding record, and very different from the original version.

These two songs were released as the two sides of Elvis's first record. It was new and exciting music, a combination of country and blues bursting with youthful energy and zest. This was rock 'n' roll.

The disc, numbered Sun 209, wasn't the first rock 'n' roll record. No one is sure what that is, but musicians had been experimenting with a combination of blues and country since the forties, and there were several other singers of Elvis's age who were making similar music at the time. But his record was to be all-important because it provided the focal point for all the others.

As Scotty Moore said later, "When Elvis busted through, it enabled all those other groups that had been going along more or less the same avenue—I'm sure there were hundreds

Left: *Elvis's first record for Sun*. Right: *Sam Phillips.*

of them—to focus on what was going to be popular. If they had a steel guitar, they dropped it. Weepers and slow country ballads pretty much went out of the repertoire. And what was left was country-orientated boogie music!"

Elvis inevitably gets most of the credit for his pioneering Sun debut because he developed his career so successfully afterward, but Sam, Scotty, and Bill made extremely important contributions to the sound which shouldn't be forgotten.

Scotty and Bill would fade into the background when Elvis became a big rock 'n' roll star, but for other musicians they remain legendary figures. Scotty Moore has been particularly influential with rock guitarists through the years, and his solos on Elvis's Sun records have been carefully copied note for note and used in tunes by the Beatles and many others.

Success for Elvis didn't come overnight. To sell records

in 1954 you first had to get them played on the radio, and when the single came out at the very beginning of August, Sam Phillips had a lot of problems. He went to all the Memphis radio stations and talked to the disc jockeys. Several liked the sound but said they couldn't play it. "He sounds too black," said the D.J. on one country station. "It sounds too rough and dirty," said another.

Finally he found someone who would take a chance with the record—Dewey Phillips (no relation to Sam) who had a program on station WHBQ called *Red Hot and Blue*. He was one of a few forward-looking disc jockeys who sensed that a change was coming in music and in young people's attitudes.

This was the time when segregation was being broken down in the South. Though many older white people didn't want anything to do with black people, young people were more adaptable. Dewey had discovered that white teenagers liked the sound of modern black records, and he played blues and used hipster talk. When he heard Elvis, the white singer who sounded black, he thought he was exactly the sort of new performer who would appeal to his listeners.

He was quite right. After just a few plays of "That's All Right" he was getting numerous telephone calls asking about the new singer. Dewey invited Elvis in for an interview. He was very nervous, but calmed down after chatting for a while. After fifteen minutes Elvis asked when the interview would start. "Oh, we've already done it," explained Dewey. "The microphone has been open all the time." Elvis went white with shock!

The record sold 20,000 copies in the Memphis area, partly because of radio plays and partly because of the live shows that Elvis, Scotty, and Bill were giving. At first they were confused about how they should present their act, and for a brief period they called themselves the Blue Moon Boys, and Elvis was known as the Hillbilly Cat.

As Scotty told writer Peter Guralnick, "There was no set plan other than when he went out on stage, to entertain better than anyone else on the bill. As time went by Elvis worked into a kind of routine. He may not have known what they wanted at first, but when he figured out what it was, he put it to them. We really had a good time and the crowds just kept getting bigger and bigger."

A rare photo of the young Elvis, who seems to be enjoying someone else's performance for a change.

Just as Elvis's records were different from the norm, so were his concerts. Most popular singers of the day stood still while they sang, but Elvis—mainly because he was nervous—moved around, and the more he moved, the more excited the crowds became.

Elvis later recalled how his onstage movements originated: "I was doing a show in Memphis. I came on stage and I was scared stiff. I was doing a fast-type tune, and everyone was hollering, and I didn't know what they were hollering at. Then I came off stage and my manager told me they were hollering because I was wiggling!"

Girls had screamed at pop singers before, but there had never been such a strong reaction to anyone as Elvis received. His shows were electrifying and had a strong impact and influence on other musicians.

Country singer Bob Luman remembered seeing a very early Elvis concert. "This cat came out in red pants and a green coat and a pink shirt and socks, and he had this sneer on his face and he stood behind the mike for five minutes, I'll bet, before he made a move. Then he hit his guitar a lick and broke two strings! I'd been playing ten years and I hadn't broken a total of two strings. He made chills run up my back. That's the last time I tried to sing like Webb Pierce and Lefty Frizzell."

Scotty Moore was Elvis's first manager, arranging show bookings and transportation, but when things started to get hectic, Bob Neal (the disc jockey from the *High Noon Roundup* show) took over. Neal worked with Elvis for about a year as his popularity grew spectacularly with each concert and record release.

Four more singles were released on Sun, in 1955, and the pattern of a blues song on one side and a country song on the other was repeated with each. "Good Rockin' Tonight," one of the most popular numbers from Elvis's live

31

shows, was released in January, with an exhilarating version of the country tune "I Don't Care If the Sun Don't Shine." In February a single of "Milk Cow Blues" and "You're a Heartbreaker" was released.

Elvis had now had three records released, and all sold well in the Memphis area. Then the national music business magazines began to notice the singer with "the distinctive new style." The fourth single appeared in May, "Baby, Let's Play House" and "I'm Right, You're Left, She's Gone," which made the national country Top 10. The fifth single, "Mystery Train" and "I Forgot to Remember to Forget," was released in July, and by autumn it was a number 1 country hit.

According to Marion Keisker, recording Elvis was never straightforward or easy. "He didn't write his own songs, and he didn't rehearse. First thing, he'd always want to cover some records he heard on the jukebox. And Sam would have to persuade him he couldn't do that."

Sam Phillips seems to have had a special skill at handling musicians and bringing the best out of them. "I went with the idea that an artist should have something not just good, but totally unique," he explained. "When I found someone like that I did everything in my power to bring it out." Which is exactly what he did with Elvis, for a series of energetic and exciting records which some rock 'n' roll enthusiasts insist Elvis never bettered.

But the going in the early days was not always easy or smooth. Elvis made one appearance on the *Grand Ole Opry*, a live country show that was broadcast over the radio each Saturday evening. It was not very successful, and one of the stagehands told him he should go back to driving trucks. "Elvis cried all the way home," one of his musician friends recalled. "It took him weeks to get over it."

But another radio show appearance was much more

No photographs were taken of Elvis, Scotty Moore, and Bill Black inside the Sun studio, but they are pictured together here in a scene from the movie Jailhouse Rock.

successful; this was the *Louisiana Hayride,* and Elvis signed to perform regularly for a year. He was nervous in the beginning, but grew much more confident over the weeks and read out advertisements as well as singing.

Elvis and his band were booked for concerts farther and farther afield. His musicians now included a drummer, D. J. Fontana, whom he'd met at *Louisiana Hayride.* They traveled to shows in Scotty Moore's large car. Bob Neal often came, too, and would warm up the audience by telling jokes.

Elvis was becoming a star and was away from home for long periods, but he never forgot his beloved parents. Gladys still worried about him, and she couldn't go to sleep at night unless he telephoned her. He remembered to call every night.

He was still a very shy, quiet person. Bob Neal said that he was an ideal act to manage; he was punctual, polite, and never big-headed. But though bashful offstage, he changed dramatically in front of a crowd, when he became a ball of energy.

Neal remembers that right from the start Elvis was very ambitious and determined to be successful. "He threw everything into it. He was greatly anxious of success. He talked not in terms of being a moderate success. No, his ambition was to be big in movies and so forth."

Elvis's subsequent fame and fortune had a lot to do not only with his enormous determination to succeed, but also because he linked up with a new manager who was equally ambitious, Colonel Tom Parker.

Bob Neal had booked Elvis on a country music package tour in the summer of 1955. The star of the show was Hank Snow, who was managed by Colonel Tom. Presley was less well known than any of the other performers, but none of them, not even Snow, were prepared to go onstage after him. His act was so exciting that anything which followed was an anticlimax.

Parker was very interested in this young performer and became involved with his career. He met Vernon and Gladys several times and helped Bob book Elvis for shows in several states in the South.

Bob Neal's contract with Elvis didn't run out until March 1956, but the Colonel was becoming increasingly involved in Elvis's management and by the autumn of 1955 he had virtually taken over.

Parker had a great deal of experience in promotion. He was born in June 1910, though there is some confusion about his early years. He has claimed to have been born Thomas Andrew Parker in the United States, but Presley biographer Albert Goldman has asserted that his birthplace was Holland, his real name was Andreas Cornelis van Kuijk, and that he came to America by boat when he was eighteen, changed his name, and, after a spell in the U.S. army, worked with traveling carnivals and circuses.

These were the days of the Great Depression, when many people were unemployed and there was little spare money available for leisure activities, like visiting the circus. Tom learned that he had to be clever if he wanted to survive. He became known as a crafty and successful small businessman. When the circus was losing money because so few people were coming to the shows, there was a meeting to discuss lowering the seat prices. Tom had a different idea. He suggested doubling the ticket prices, but displaying a large sign reading HALF YOUR MONEY BACK IF NOT SATISFIED. This sign attracted lots more customers, all of whom pretended they weren't satisfied and asked for half their money back. But business was much better.

Tom had other stunts that he would boast about in later years, when he was managing Elvis. One involved catching sparrows and painting them yellow, then displaying them as "exotic canaries"; another was advertising "foot-long hot dogs" which had small pieces of meat at the ends, while the middle was cheap filling. When people complained, Tom would point to a piece of meat he'd dropped onto the sawdust floor earlier in the day and say, "There, you dropped your meat, boy, now move along, please."

At about the same time Elvis was born, Tom moved from the world of circuses to managing and promoting the careers of country singers. He was very successful at his job. He had great skill at advance publicity. A day or two before his singers were due in town, he'd arrive and place posters everywhere. He was also very successful at getting good money for his singers.

In 1953 he was made an honorary colonel by the governor of Tennessee. The name suited the large, ambitious man with the big reputation. He was perhaps the only person who realized just how successful Elvis could be. "When I first heard this boy," he told a San Diego, California, newspaper, "I detected a sensitivity and a talent that is boundless. This boy will go far."

Parker also realized that if Elvis was to fulfill his potential, there would have to be some dramatic changes. First, though Sam Phillips had helped Elvis and his music enormously, the Sun label was too small. Tom decided that Presley should sign with one of the large, international record companies. Second, he realized that Elvis could make much more money if his business affairs were carefully organized from the beginning, and if he could have his own publishing company handling the royalties from all the songs he would record.

Soon Parker began negotiating with big record companies. He approached several and asked for previously unheard-of sums of money for a singer's contract.

Tom's old friend Steve Sholes at RCA was very interested and eventually offered Sam Phillips $35,000 for Elvis and all the records that he made for Sun. At the time it was an unprecedented sum for a new singer, and Sam accepted because he needed the money. He believed that there were many singers in the Memphis area who were as talented as Elvis, and he decided to take the money to boost their careers. When Carl Perkins, Jerry Lee Lewis, and Johnny Cash had big hits with Sun, Sam would point to their success as justification for accepting the RCA deal. But millions of dollars were made by RCA as a result of signing Elvis, and as the years passed, it became obvious that Sam Phillips had received a very poor deal.

RCA paid Elvis a bonus of $5,000, and he used some of the money to buy his first car—a pink Cadillac, which he gave to Gladys, even though she couldn't drive and didn't have a license.

Elvis with Johnny Cash, another Sun recording artist.

At about the same time a company called Elvis Presley Music was set up by Parker to publish all the songs that Presley would record. It was a very smart business move, which would eventually add millions of dollars to Elvis's income, in addition to the royalties he would make from his records.

Colonel Tom Parker won the respect of Elvis and his parents. He showed that he could make Elvis very successful and very wealthy. They were pleased to allow him control of Elvis's career. Few men have ever had such a successful working relationship. Parker devoted himself to promoting Elvis's career, working incredibly hard and, in the process, earning himself an enormous amount of money.

Elvis with Norma Baker, a fan, in Nashville, Tennessee, in 1956.

4

Fame and Fortune

The last few months of 1955 involved some overlap between Elvis's agreements with Sun and RCA, and with Bob Neal and Colonel Parker. It was the end of the first phase of his career, where he'd proved his tremendous ability as a rock 'n' roll performer, and the start of the second, a two-year period where he revealed enormous potential as a money earner—from records, music publishing, TV appearances, and films.

But in October 1955 his fame was largely confined to the South, and to country fans in particular. That month he performed in Nashville, Tennessee, at the Country and Western Disc Jockey Convention, and the assembled D.J.'s voted him the Most Promising Newcomer of the Year.

At the same time he had three songs on the country music charts: "Baby, Let's Play House" and both sides of the fifth Sun single, "Mystery Train" and "I Forgot to Remember to Forget."

This situation obviously pleased RCA, but they planned to make records with Elvis that would sell to record buyers well beyond the country market. Unlike Sam Phillips's company, which was small, had limited funds to spend on publicity, and had to depend on independent organizations around the country to distribute records, RCA was international, with many employees, a lot of money, and the ability to get records into every shop in the United States

An early RCA publicity photograph, taken during one of Elvis's first recording sessions with the company.

and many countries abroad. By joining RCA, Elvis was moving into the big time.

Popular music was then dominated by smartly dressed, conventional-looking men and women who stood still by the microphone while they sang, and smiled pleasantly at their audiences. Most of the biggest hits of 1955 had been as sedate as their titles suggest: "Sincerely," "Love Is a Many Splendored Thing," and "Cherry Pink and Apple Blossom White." It was hardly surprising that a rock 'n' roll singer wearing outrageous clothes, dancing wildly around the microphone, and snarling at the audience would make quite an impact.

The first successful rock 'n' roll act had been Bill Haley and the Comets. In the summer of 1955, while Presley was still touring small towns in Tennessee and Texas, Haley's "Rock Around the Clock" was the top-selling record in America for eight weeks. Bill Haley was a country singer who sensed the movement in musical fashion and changed to singing blues songs in a fast, country-oriented style. The music was fresh and exciting, but it was more than ten years since Bill Haley had been a teenager, and when Elvis and other energetic young rock 'n' rollers came to national attention, Haley slipped from popularity.

On January 10, 1956, two days after celebrating his twenty-first birthday, Elvis drove from Memphis to Nashville with Colonel Tom and his assistant, Tom Diskin, to make his first recordings for RCA.

The two-day session was masterminded by Steve Sholes, the RCA man who had signed Elvis to the label, and Chet Atkins, a musician who was in charge of RCA's newly opened Nashville office.

The band was made up of Scotty and Bill, who'd been the only musicians on the Sun records, drummer D. J.

Fontana, Chet Atkins on guitar, pianist Floyd Cramer, and three male backup singers known as the Jordanaires. All would work with Elvis on many subsequent recording sessions.

The sound on the RCA discs was different from the Sun records. As music critics have pointed out ever since, much of the roughness and raw energy that made the Memphis recordings so unique was lost forever. There were various reasons: The extra musicians and singers made the sound fuller and smoother; Elvis was changing and maturing as a vocalist; and Steve Sholes was deliberately trying to make the sound as commercial as possible so that it would appeal to a wide audience. He succeeded, and the records, if not as "wild and free" as the classics from 1954 and 1955, were still very exciting and different from most of the other popular music of the day.

The RCA studios in Nashville were nearly as primitive as Sam Phillips's studio in Memphis, but they did have the extra facility of an old stairwell that created an unusual echo effect. Elvis sang the vocal for "Heartbreak Hotel" there, one of the five songs recorded at the session.

"Heartbreak Hotel" was his first RCA release and the dramatic, echoing vocals helped to make it a number 1 hit around the world, selling millions of copies. It's still regarded, by Elvis fans worldwide, as one of the finest recordings he ever made. It marked another change from Elvis's previous recordings, because "Heartbreak Hotel" wasn't an old country or blues tune, but a new composition by songwriters Mae Boren Axton and Tommy Durden.

After the two days of recording there were more concert dates in the South, and then came a trip to New York City to appear on a live television variety show starring bandleaders Tommy and Jimmy Dorsey. Their show was doing badly in the TV ratings and Elvis was booked for

Presley's live performances became wilder and wilder.

five appearances to try and attract more viewers.

Nothing like Elvis's performance had been seen on TV screens before. The infamous wiggle, first done onstage in Memphis because he was nervous, was now an important part of the act. He was aggressive with his guitar, swinging his arm down so that his fingers snapped at the strings, and he snarled playfully at the cameras as he sang two rock 'n' roll numbers, "Heartbreak Hotel" and "Blue Suede Shoes."

Between the first and second TV shows, Elvis went into RCA's studios in New York for more recordings, including new versions of rock 'n' roll songs recently recorded by black singers, like Little Richard's "Tutti Frutti." He also taped "Blue Suede Shoes," which was written by Carl Perkins, whose own version of the song would be Sun Records' first national hit, in the summer of 1956.

The TV shows were very successful because of Elvis's

appearances. The single of "Heartbreak Hotel" entered the charts on March 24, 1956, and rose to number 1.

Steve Sholes told an interviewer that he was delighted with Elvis and the records he had made. "He's not only a good rock 'n' roll singer. He does an excellent job on ballads. Although he doesn't read music, he has a fantastically good ear and an uncanny ability to pick the right tunes. He chose 'Heartbreak Hotel' and 'Blue Suede Shoes' after hearing them once. He's also completely cooperative as an artist."

The shows frequently broke attendance records and sometimes developed into riots, as Red West, the school friend now acting as an occasional unpaid assistant to Elvis, explained about one show that got out of control.

"Elvis was wearing a bright green jacket and black pegged pants. He leaned over the edge of the stage to kiss a girl's hand. She grabbed him and tore the sleeve of his jacket. That was the signal. . . . The next thing there were girls on stage and they seemed to go berserk. They were tearing and clawing like animals. Then his shirt was torn to shreds."

Elvis enjoyed the fans' reactions to him, but his mother was understandably alarmed when she heard such stories. Asked at a press conference if he was worried by the behavior of the fans, Elvis replied, "I've never been seriously hurt. I've had my hair pulled, and a few scratches. I've lost a few suits of clothes too. But as far as I'm concerned if they want my shirt, they can have it. After all, they put it on my back to start with!"

The fans didn't confine their enthusiasm for Elvis to concerts. They would try and see him at his hotel or wherever he went. This meant that he became a virtual prisoner in hotel rooms while on tour. As he explained, "It's impossible now to leave my hotel room. I remember one night I woke up starving, but I didn't dare go out for anything. I tried it once, and the crowds were chasing me, and they smashed up an all-night delicatessen."

Colonel Tom arranged much tighter security for Elvis. After concerts he was whisked away in a car before the fans could find him and a dangerous situation could develop. Because Elvis couldn't go out and see his friends, he arranged for his friends to be with him all the time. Red West, Gene Smith (Elvis's cousin), and Lamar Fike, a very fat man who was always teased by others, were all hired to do various jobs and to be available when Elvis wanted their company.

At the same time, Parker was organizing bigger and better deals which would enable Elvis to be seen by larger audiences and to make more money, but without such a punishing schedule of concerts. Television was the perfect medium; with just one performance he could be seen by millions of people, and during 1956 Elvis made several appearances before the cameras. They increased his popularity among teenagers, but also caused a great deal of controversy among older people.

There had been criticism of Elvis's onstage movements and the wild behavior of his fans for some time, but these came to a head after two appearances on *The Milton Berle Show*, which scored ratings figures of 40 million viewers at the time "Heartbreak Hotel" was on the top of the pop charts.

It was Elvis's performance of the song "Hound Dog" on the second show that caused the greatest storm of controversy. Presley was gyrating wildly to the music while girls in the unseen studio audience screamed with delight.

Billy Graham, the best-known religious leader in the country, declared, "Elvis isn't the kind of boy I'd like my children to see," and Ed Sullivan, who had the most popular show on television, said he wouldn't touch Elvis with

Elvis onstage in Nashville in 1956.

a long pole. Several newspaper writers described Elvis as "talentless," one called him "Elvis the Pelvis," and others called him "vulgar."

Elvis was genuinely hurt and upset by some of this criticism. "I wouldn't do anything vulgar in front of anybody, especially children," he said at a press conference. "My folks didn't bring me up that way. I don't do anything bad when I work, I just move with the music, it's the way

I feel. Some people tap their feet, some people just snap their fingers, and some people just sway back and forth. I just started doing them all together."

The controversy that surrounded Elvis may seem puzzling to us these days, when so many performers use exaggerated movements when they sing, but Elvis was the first person, certainly on national television, to behave in such a manner.

Many influential people connected rock 'n' roll performers (of whom Elvis was easily the most successful and notorious) with trouble. A New York newspaper made a strong call for a "crackdown on rock 'n' roll," and the powers-that-be in the state of New Jersey banned all rock 'n' roll concerts.

In the South, segregation had just been outlawed, and people who wished the old ways to continue, with black and white separated, were the strongest opponents of the new music and musicians. They saw that people like Elvis were drawing black and white people together with their music. There were protests and public burnings of rock 'n' roll records, and some black rock 'n' roll singers were threatened and attacked.

But no one could stop the growing popularity of the music. Every controversy about Elvis meant more publicity for his records. Parker was able to ask for, and get, more money for appearances. A film contract was signed with Paramount Pictures, who realized that Elvis's popularity and fame could make him a box office draw with movie audiences.

There were more TV shows, including a famous appearance on *The Steve Allen Show*, where Elvis sang his big "Hound Dog" hit to a real dog that sat obediently on a podium, wearing a hat and looking miserable!

Then Ed Sullivan, who'd previously insisted that he

wouldn't have Elvis anywhere near his program, booked him for three shows, paying a huge fee of $50,000. The shows were watched by 54 million people, 82.6 percent of the potential viewing audience. To avoid controversy, Ed Sullivan had Elvis filmed from the waist up so that no one except the studio audience could see him wiggling.

Elvis Presley now had millions of devoted teenage fans, and they wanted to buy anything and everything to do with their hero. Colonel Parker had arranged with a company to manufacture nothing but Elvis souvenirs, and they sold hundreds of different items, including pictures, calendars, posters, pencil cases, and bubble gum.

Parker had also made contact with the various Elvis fan clubs that had been organized, and brought them all under his control. He gave the various fan club secretaries pictures and information, but was able to use them as unpaid Elvis Presley publicity officers. When a new record came out, they would be told to ask members to telephone radio stations with requests for the song to be played.

Elvis Presley was becoming an industry, and records were the most successful part of it. Everything that RCA released in 1956 sold in enormous quantities; there were eleven singles, six EPs, and two LPs. (EP stands for "extended play," meaning a phonograph record of 45 rpm that plays longer than the standard 45 rpm record.) In the United States he had four number 1 singles: "Heartbreak Hotel," "Don't Be Cruel," "Love Me Tender," and "Hound Dog." It was a similar story in other countries, though sometimes different records were released; in England "Blue Suede Shoes" was a number 1 hit. The first LP, Elvis Presley, was a top seller in America for ten weeks; the second, Elvis, entered the LP chart at number 1 and stayed on the listings for thirty-two weeks.

The recording sessions that produced these hits were

unusual. Most singers planned what they were going to record before they went into the studio, but not Elvis. His decisions were made on the spot, usually as a response to demonstration discs that had been specially prepared by people with a similar style.

An Otis Blackwell song was used as the title for Elvis's first film, *Love Me Tender*. It had originally been intended to call the film *The Reno Brothers*, but Paramount realized that they could get some valuable free publicity if the film was named after one of Elvis's big hits.

Elvis went to Hollywood, California, to make the film in August 1956. Several of his Memphis friends, including Red West and Lamar Fike, went along to keep him company, and in later films they would be used for small parts and as stunt men.

Presley enjoyed making movies and seems to have impressed the filmmakers with his politeness and professionalism. He pleased the director of *Love Me Tender* on the very first day when he revealed that he'd learned not just his own lines, but everyone else's as well!

The film was set at the end of the Civil War, and Elvis played Clint Reno, the youngest of four brothers. He dies at the end of the film, which apparently upset his mother a great deal when she went to see a preview in Memphis.

Love Me Tender was to be the first of a string of very successful films for Elvis. The costs were recovered within a week of its release. Few movies in Hollywood history have made their money back quite so fast. The fans loved it, and some saw it many times; but the film critics gave it generally unfavorable reviews, several saying that Elvis couldn't act.

He was now making a lot of money and was able to buy a new home for his parents at 1034 Audubon Drive, Memphis. His father gave up his job and began to help

Elvis with his business affairs. Fans found out about the new house and created all kinds of problems trying to get Elvis's autograph (when he was in town) or searching for souvenirs—including the washing hung on the line!

Elvis's parents don't seem to have changed much, didn't acquire expensive tastes, and still visited their old friends at Lauderdale Court. Gladys was very pleased at Elvis's success, but apparently wished he would retire from show business, invest his money in a shop, and settle down with a wife, though she never told her son this.

Organizing a private life was a problem for Elvis. He couldn't go to stores or to the movies without causing a minor riot, so he began making special arrangements in Memphis, like hiring a theater or a roller-skating rink from midnight on. He also rented the local fairground when it was closed to the public, and he and his friends would ride the bumper cars and the roller coaster until dawn.

Elvis was under tremendous pressure, though he seldom showed the strain in public. A rare exception came when he appeared on a local New York TV show, *Hy Gardner Calling*. Elvis, who looked tired and worn out, was asked how success was affecting him, and he replied, "It's affected my sleep. I average about four or five hours a night. Everything has happened to me so fast in the last year and a half, I'm all mixed up. I can't keep up with everything that's happening."

The interview provided one of the few indications that Elvis was perhaps too successful for his own good. Every step he took brought more fame and wealth. He had wanted to be famous, but could never have expected quite how big he would become, nor could he explain why he had done so well so suddenly. Questioned by *The Saturday Evening Post* in 1956, he said, "I don't know what it is. I just fell into it really. My dad and I were laughing about it the other day. He looked at me and said, 'What happened, Elvis? The last thing I remember is, I was working in a factory and you were driving a truck.' "

Elvis's only explanation was that he'd been very lucky. "I came along at a time in the music business when there was no trend. The people were looking for something different and I just came along in time."

He had arrived at an opportune moment. It was the time when breakable 78 rpm records were being replaced with unbreakable 45 rpm records, which were smaller and could be produced and distributed more cheaply; it was the time when inexpensive record-playing equipment was becoming available; and it was a time when teenagers had more spare money than ever before.

His success had revolutionized the music industry; he'd dramatically increased the audience for popular music, made radio stations change the format of their programs to feature rock 'n' roll singers, and prompted hundreds of other young singers to try and equal his achievements. As Buddy Holly, a great rock 'n' roll singer from Texas, said, "Without Elvis, none of us could have made it."

Many people tried to cash in on his success, and there were several novelty records that featured his name in the title, including "Elvis for President" and "My Boy Elvis."

But the most successful person at making money from the Elvis name remained Colonel Tom Parker, and he seems to have made only one mistake in 1956. He booked Elvis for a two-week engagement in Las Vegas, a neon-lit city in the Nevada desert, which was a popular center for gambling. Most customers didn't enjoy the shows, the second week of concerts was canceled, and Elvis came home early.

With the exception of these shows, 1956 was a very successful year for Elvis, very busy and full of controversy.

The success story continued in 1957, but his workload was reduced, and there was far less criticism from public figures and newspapers.

Ed Sullivan led the way for the older generation, to start accepting Elvis and not criticize him, when Elvis appeared on his TV show again. He embarrassed Elvis by coming out after he'd sung "Don't Be Cruel" and announcing, "I wanted to say to Elvis Presley and the country that this is a real decent fine boy, and we've never had a pleasanter experience on our show with a big name than we've had with him."

Further proof that Elvis wasn't an evil influence came when RCA released a new EP featuring his favorite religious songs, entitled *Peace in the Valley*. The record wasn't released to help improve his image, though, because Elvis had long wanted to make such a record. Almost every recording session began with impromptu gospel singing to help Elvis and his musicians get in the right mood.

There were fewer riots in 1957, but that was because there were fewer concerts, not because the fans were becoming more restrained. The Colonel had deliberately cut down on the number of Elvis's personal appearances because he feared that Elvis was in danger of overexposure.

With more time on his hands Elvis went looking for a bigger and better house for his family. In March he bought a large 23-room mansion in the suburb of Whitehaven, south of Memphis. It was called Graceland and cost $100,000.

Elvis moved in with his parents and grandmother and began to arrange for the remodeling of several rooms and the construction of a kidney-shaped swimming pool.

Two more Elvis films were released in 1957, and they surpassed the box office success of *Love Me Tender*. *Loving*

Elvis takes a break during the filming of Loving You.

You was a movie with the familiar-sounding plot of a truck driver who becomes a successful rock 'n' roll singer. It is the only Elvis film with performances that were anything like his concerts. Later films were increasingly aimed at a family audience and contained none of the controversial stage movements of the fifties.

Jailhouse Rock was also about a man who found fame and fortune when he made a record, though this character was mean and tough, and the film opened with Elvis being sent to jail for accidentally killing a man. The title song from

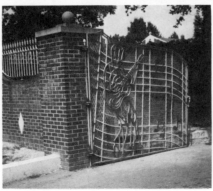

Top: *Graceland was set on several acres and surrounded by high walls.* Left: *Elvis's extensive remodeling of the estate included "musical" gates.*

Jailhouse Rock is used in the best production number from any of Presley's many films and features Elvis with several gyrating jailbirds.

"Jailhouse Rock" and "Teddy Bear" (from *Loving You*) were two of Elvis's biggest hits of the year. His fans around the world sent hundreds of teddy bears to their hero when the record was released. Elvis was pleased, but also astonished that people should do such things.

The year 1957 ended with a sensation for the fans. Elvis received his draft notice from the U.S. Army on December 10. In those days every young American male was eligible to be called up for two years in the armed services. Elvis had been given a medical examination earlier in the year and was declared fit, but it wasn't expected that he'd be called up until late in 1958.

The prospect of Elvis disappearing from the public eye appalled the fans, and the Memphis draft board received hundreds of angry and threatening messages. Desperate pleas were made to Colonel Tom Parker to use his influence to keep Elvis out of the army.

5

Elvis in the Army

Elvis Presley's millions of fans weren't the only people shocked and dismayed to hear that he was going into the army for two years. As the most successful entertainer in history, he was making fortunes for many others besides himself, and people in the record and film worlds were concerned at the large sums they'd lose if Elvis disappeared. Two years is a long time in the music business; they feared he would be forgotten by the fans, and that sales of records and interest in his films would fall dramatically.

But the Colonel doesn't seem to have been particularly worried. He was very confident that Elvis would always be popular, and he made plans to insure that the Presley name wouldn't be forgotten by the fans. He also realized that Elvis didn't want to hear suggestions about avoiding a spell of army duty.

Elvis considered himself a loyal citizen, proud to receive

a draft notice and proud to be able to serve his country. As he told reporters, "It's a duty I've got to fill, and I'm gonna do it." Only the thought of being away from his beloved mother, Gladys, seemed to have worried him. "I guess the only thing I'll hate about it is leaving mama. She's always been my best girl."

He then explained that he didn't want to be treated differently from the other young men he'd be serving with. This surprised everyone, including the army, who'd expected Elvis to apply for enlistment in the Special Services, the unit in which many popular entertainers served. It would have made his two-year army career much easier because most of his work would have involved singing and performing at concerts for fellow soldiers in various parts of the world and would have meant a lot of time off.

But Elvis was determined to be a normal soldier, even though it would involve hard work, long hours, and perhaps dangerous missions. It would be a dramatic contrast from his show business life as the King of Rock 'n' Roll.

The Colonel gave Elvis his full support and made it clear to everyone concerned that for two years Elvis would be a soldier and not a singer. There might be recording sessions when he was on leave, but there would be no concerts, and that rule included any special events the army wanted to organize.

Parker was already planning the future—he saw that Elvis could become popular with all ages and that a career in the army would help toward that end. If he was seen as a brave, patriotic citizen who hadn't tried to get out of a difficult job, he would win the respect of many people, including those who had once criticized his "vulgar" movements onstage.

Elvis was probably thinking the same way too. When reporters asked what he thought would happen in two years' time, he replied, "I hope my fans will welcome me back. Maybe I'll start a new career as a ballad singer, or a singer of spirituals."

The draft notice, delivered on December 20, 1957, called on Elvis to report for duty on January 20, 1958. This gave him only a month to get ready, and took everyone by surprise, particularly Paramount Pictures, the film company that had spent a lot of money preparing for the next Elvis movie, *King Creole*.

Paramount begged the Colonel to do something to change the call-up date, and he asked Elvis to write a letter. It was typically polite and asked for a delay. He pointed out that he wasn't asking for himself, but for the film people who'd lose a lot of money if *King Creole* was canceled or postponed.

The request was granted and he was given an extra sixty days in which to make the film. *King Creole* was about a young man who becomes a popular singer in a New Orleans nightclub but gets mixed up with some violent criminals. As with the earlier Elvis pictures, it was largely filmed in Hollywood studios, but some shots were filmed on location in New Orleans itself. Elvis was very popular in this city, and an Elvis Presley Day was declared and all the local children were given the day off from school.

There were remarkable scenes as thousands of enthusiastic young fans tried to catch a glimpse of their hero, and the film crew had a difficult time getting any work done.

When *King Creole* was completed, Elvis prepared for the army. As he told reporters, "My induction notice says for me to leave my car at home. Transportation will be provided. They tell me just to bring a razor, a toothbrush, a comb, and enough money to hold me two weeks."

Elvis did just as he was told, arriving at the Memphis

draft board office at 6:30 in the morning on Monday, March 24, 1958. He came with his parents and a few friends, who'd been up all night at a going-away party.

Several fans had woken up early to bid a tearful farewell to Elvis, and the Colonel was there giving away free balloons advertising the forthcoming film. He'd also arranged for photographers and reporters to be present. For the next few days Parker would use the press to get as much publicity for Elvis as possible; the army didn't seem to mind, because the publicity was good for them, too, and would encourage other young men to join the army.

Elvis was given a medical test, sworn in, and then given his army number, US 53310761. His pay would be $78 a month, a dramatic drop from the $100,000 a month he'd been getting from RCA in 1957!

A bus took Private Presley and the other new recruits

Left: *Private Presley on the move.* Right: *A photograph for the fans.*

from Memphis to Fort Chaffee, Arkansas. When they stopped briefly for a break at a restaurant, they were besieged by fans and had to leave hurriedly.

After a night at Fort Chaffee, Elvis and the other new recruits awoke for breakfast to discover that the place was overrun with reporters and photographers. The biggest event of the day for them was going to be Elvis's haircut.

Every soldier in the army had to have a crew cut. Elvis paid 65 cents to the barber, James Peterson, and then grinned as the man cut his famous hair and removed the sideburns. No one was allowed to keep the hair; it was mixed with that of the other soldiers and thrown away. Fans waiting outside who'd hoped for a lock of the hair were disappointed.

The next day Elvis was issued a uniform and there was a press conference. He was going to Fort Hood in Texas for basic training. Everyone had nice things to say about the new soldier. "I believe the army has shown that it is trying to make an ordinary soldier out of Mr. Presley," a general explained. "He has been afforded no special privileges and he has conducted himself in a marvelous manner."

The press reporters followed Elvis all the way to Fort Hood. There, the army decided to call a halt to all the publicity. The reporters went away, but the fans didn't give up so easily. They stayed outside in the hope of catching sight of Elvis. Every weekend of Elvis's stay at the fort, there would be fans camped outside. He received two thousand letters in his first week, and there were hundreds of phone calls.

By all accounts Elvis settled into the army very quickly. He really did get treated the same way as the other soldiers, worked hard, and even used some of his spare time to improve his pistol shooting.

It was announced that he'd have eight weeks' basic training, two weeks' leave, another fourteen weeks' training, then would be transferred, with other soldiers, to serve in West Germany.

Elvis had been in the recording studios before he began his army service, and RCA was planning to spread new releases over several months. On his two weeks' leave he made more recordings and went to the Memphis opening of *King Creole,* which brought some encouraging "Elvis can act" comments in the newspapers.

For the second phase of training at Fort Hood, Elvis lived outside the camp with his parents, in a three-bedroom trailer that he'd bought. The army allowed any soldier with relatives living nearby to live with them.

He lived there for two months, but then his mother, who'd been ill for some time, took a turn for the worse. She found it difficult to concentrate on anything and was having trouble walking. Elvis drove her back to Memphis and arranged for private treatment at the new Methodist Hospital. He was determined that she should have the best medical attention he could buy.

Gladys had bravely coped with ill health for years and had struggled out to work to provide for her family when most people would have stayed in bed. Her health problems were largely caused by her weight. She liked fattening foods and was overweight, so she took diet pills, but they made her very weak and put pressure on her heart.

The doctors at Methodist Hospital diagnosed hepatitis, a liver infection. Three days later she became seriously ill and Vernon sent an urgent message to Fort Hood for Elvis to return home immediately. He was given emergency leave and rushed to her bedside.

Two days later, on August 14, 1958, she had a heart attack and died. She was just forty-six. Elvis was heartbroken. "Oh, God, oh, God, everything I have is gone" was his grief-stricken comment.

The funeral of Gladys Presley took place at Graceland with 400 invited guests; 3,000 sad-eyed Elvis fans came to pay their respects and stood silently outside the gates.

Gladys had shared her son's love for gospel music, and her favorite gospel group was the Blackwoods, so Elvis hired a special plane to bring them to the funeral to sing.

After the service her body was taken with a procession of cars to Forest Hill Cemetery, three miles away. Above her grave stood a life-size statue of Jesus with arms out-stretched. The inscription on the gravestone read:

> Gladys Smith Presley
> April 25, 1912—August 14, 1958
> Beloved wife of Vernon Presley and mother
> of Elvis Presley
> She was the sunshine of our home

Elvis returned to Texas on August 24, telling reporters at the Dallas airport, "One of the last things Mom said was that Dad and I should always be together. I'll report back to Fort Hood in the morning. Wherever they send me, Dad will go too." Elvis followed Gladys's wishes—Vernon would seldom be far from his son over the next nineteen years. When he learned where he'd be stationed in Germany, Elvis made plans for his father and grand-mother and some members of his Memphis entourage to come too.

Elvis took the train to New York in September 1958. He was going to Europe by boat with 1,400 other soldiers. Before he left, there was a press conference, and Steve Sholes at RCA had arranged to record it for an EP called "Elvis Sails."

The Press Interviews Elvis

RCA VICTOR
4SEP EPA-5157
LATE

LATE
EXTRA
ELVIS SAILS

Top: *After a stint in the army Elvis made the film* G.I. Blues, *in which he played a soldier.* Left: *The "interview" record.*

"Do the other soldiers give you a rough time because you're famous?" asked one reporter.

"No, sir, I was very surprised," said Elvis. "I've never met a nicer group of boys in my life. They probably would have if it had been like everybody thought, that I wouldn't have to work and been given special treatment."

In reply to a question about his mother he explained, "Everybody loves their mother, but I was an only child and my mother was always with me, all my life. It was like losing a friend, a companion, someone to talk to. I could wake her at any hour of the day or night if I was troubled by something."

What would Elvis do if rock 'n' roll died? "I'd probably starve to death," he joked. "If it ever did happen, and I don't think it would, I'd make a serious try to keep on top in movies."

Was Elvis looking forward to Germany? "Well, I'm kinda looking forward to it. Just before I came in the army we were going to tour Europe. I get quite a bit of mail from there." There were a few more questions, then the army band played some of his hits and Elvis got aboard the troopship USS *Randall*.

The German fans turned out in force for his arrival, and the local press was given three days to take all the pictures they wanted before Elvis got on with his assigned duty as a "scout" jeep driver.

He drove an army sergeant around, searching out routes for tanks if there were ever an emergency. They had to know the roads well and spent a lot of time traveling.

Vernon and Elvis's grandmother, Minnie Mae, arrived from the United States and lived with Elvis in a hotel; then he rented a house. Lamar Fike and Red West also arrived. Two secretaries were hired to deal with the mountains of mail brought every morning.

The house was often besieged by fans, and a notice was put on the front door saying "Autographs between 7:30 and 8:30 only" to try and stop people from knocking at the door all day long. Elvis couldn't go out much in his off-duty hours and usually ate at home. "My grandmother cooks all my favorite dishes," he explained. "You know, good simple food just like my mama used to make."

Back home the fans hadn't forgotten Elvis, as many had feared. He had several hits with songs recorded before he entered the army, including "Hard Headed Woman," "King Creole" (the film was released during the school summer holidays and was very successful), "A Fool Such As I," and "Big Hunk of Love."

When the new recordings ran out, older material was repackaged onto LPs. In February 1959 *For LP Fans Only* was released and included some material from the Sun days; and in August 1959 *A Date with Elvis* appeared, which featured more of the Sun recordings and songs from the first two films.

RCA and the Colonel were pleased when both records went into the Top 10. It suggested that there were many Elvis fans who would buy all his records, regardless of whether they had some, or all, of the songs featured. Over the years Elvis records would be repackaged many times, and the most devoted fans had several copies of the same recordings, but in different LP collections. They were encouraged in their purchases by the inclusion of special extras, like posters and calendars. *A Date with Elvis* has a signed message from Elvis, written in Germany.

The Colonel kept up interest in Elvis by releasing various stories to the newspapers. These included plans for his return from the army, and though some didn't materialize, it was all good publicity.

The highlight of his stay in Europe seems to have been a trip to Paris, when he had a few days' leave. French fans weren't informed of his visit and he was able to walk the streets and go into shops and restaurants. As he later explained, "It reminded me of the life I used to live, before I joined the service. I loved Paris. I didn't have to sign too many autographs, and I became an ordinary guy for a while. I enjoyed the break and needed a rest."

At a club he was recognized by waiters, and after the audience had gone home, he gave an impromptu performance, singing some songs. It was the first time he'd given a show of any kind in eighteen months, and the only occasion he performed when he was in the army.

There were three things that happened in Germany that would have important effects on his life. A demonstration of karate, a sport that would become an obsession for him, an introduction to pills that change sleep patterns, and a meeting with Priscilla Beaulieu, the woman he would marry in 1967.

His interest in karate grew quickly and he became very good at it, winning a second dan black belt. Back in Memphis he would introduce the sport to all his friends, and in the seventies he introduced karate movements into his stage act.

The drug-taking started when he had to stay up all night

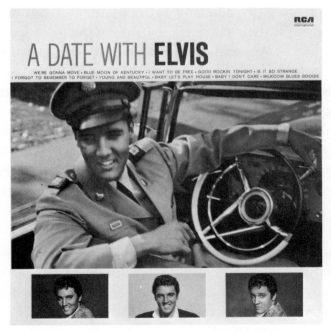

RCA continued to issue new Elvis records while he was away from the music scene.

with other soldiers while on maneuvers. They had to stay awake and be on their toes, so a sergeant gave Elvis and some others a drug called Dexedrine, which helps you stay awake. Elvis was impressed with the drug's effects and, according to Red West, began taking it regularly when he was back home. He was perhaps unaware that the drug could be very dangerous if misused or taken over a long period. Later, drugs like Dexedrine would have a very damaging effect on his health.

Priscilla Beaulieu was the daughter of an American air force captain, and she was just fourteen when she first met Elvis. By all accounts he was entranced by the mature young teenager. He met several women in Germany, but Priscilla was the one who made the most lasting impression. Back in America he'd say, "She is very mature, very intelligent, and the most beautiful girl I've ever seen, but there's no romance, it's nothing serious."

Vernon Presley also met his second wife in Germany. Davada Elliott, better known as Dee, was then married to an army sergeant.

In January 1960, just before the end of his tour of duty, Elvis was promoted to sergeant. Back home, the Colonel was making plans for his return, the highlight of which would be a TV special with Frank Sinatra, a very popular singer with the older generation, who'd once been very critical of rock 'n' roll but had changed his opinion when he got to know more about Elvis.

The day before Elvis's flight to America there was a press conference, and he was astonished to find that one of the people involved with the organization was Marion Keisker, the woman from Sun Records who'd first recognized his talent. She was now Captain Keisker in the U.S. Army, working with Armed Forces Television in Germany. Elvis was thrilled to see her, hugging her and telling people, "You wouldn't be having this thing today if it wasn't for this lady!"

He was asked similar questions to the ones he'd been asked before he sailed to Germany, proudly displayed his army Certificate of Achievement, and, when asked about the future, replied, "I'm gonna let my sideburns grow a little, but I doubt if they'll be as long as they were. I've gotten over that kick. I'll just continue doing what comes naturally. I don't consider the new crop of singers as rivals. I've always believed that there's room in show business for everyone. I don't know about marriage. I guess I'll wait until the bug bites, and it hasn't yet."

Priscilla was at the airport to see him off, and the news-paper headlines described her as "The girl he left behind." Back in the United States, there were more press confer-ences, then on March 5, 1960, he was discharged and became a civilian again. He went home to Graceland for a rest.

6

The

Film Years

Elvis's return was a big story for the American newspapers. The Nashville-based *Music Reporter* described his landing at a New Jersey air force base in a snowstorm and commented, "Despite his two years of obscurity serving with the U.S. Army in Germany, Presley's worldwide fame seemed to have gathered force in the interim."

There was a large crowd welcoming him back to Memphis, and the local police had put a guard on the gates at Graceland. It was March, but there was still a decorated Christmas tree in the house, kept to show Elvis, because Christmas was his favorite time of the year. He enjoyed being at Graceland for the holiday, and he'd been forced to miss it two years running.

"Graceland is full of memories for me. Maybe that's what makes it home," he said. He began making plans to remodel parts of the house, and he increased the size of his staff. Old Memphis friends were back on the payroll, as were two friends he'd met in the army, Joe Esposito and Charlie Hodge.

On March 20 Elvis traveled to Nashville to make some new records. There were advance orders for one million copies of his next single, and he hadn't even decided what song it should be, let alone recorded it! RCA had printed a special bag for the disc and was just waiting to stamp on the title so they could rush copies into the shops.

RCA's Nashville studios had been considerably improved in Elvis's absence, and the sound of the early sixties records, produced by Chet Atkins and Steve Sholes, was of a particularly high quality.

The musicians at the session would make up the core of his band for the next few years, including Scotty Moore (but not Bill Black, who was now fronting his own successful band, the Bill Black Combo); pianist Floyd Cramer; guitarist Hank Garland; two drummers, D. J. Fontana and Buddy Harmon; and the Jordanaires. The all-night session produced "Stuck on You" and "Fame and Fortune," the two sides of his new hit record.

The next day Elvis went to Miami, Florida, to appear on the Frank Sinatra TV special. The Colonel had arranged the guest appearance, confident that it would provide enormous publicity for Elvis and his new record.

Frank Sinatra was the first of many who'd criticized Elvis in the fifties but would praise him in the sixties. In 1957 he'd described rock 'n' roll as "phony and false, and sung, written, and played for the most part by cretinous goons," but he'd clearly changed his mind, certainly about Elvis, as he gave him a very warm welcome.

As expected, both the TV show and the new record did extremely well. It proved that Elvis was still "the King," the most popular and successful entertainer in the world. Surprisingly no one had emerged during his enforced ab-

Top: A rare "off duty" picture of Elvis, taken at Graceland one Christmas. Bottom: Elvis's first public appearance after his discharge from the army, in a TV special with Frank Sinatra.

sence to successfully challenge his popularity. Most of the stars who'd been big in 1957 and 1958 were gone from the charts, and none of the newcomers showed any signs of being as big as Elvis.

The great names of fifties rock 'n' roll had met a variety of fates. Buddy Holly and Eddie Cochran had been killed in accidents, Chuck Berry had dropped out of sight, the career of Jerry Lee Lewis had slumped following the widespread news coverage of his marriage to his thirteen-year-old cousin, Little Richard had given up rock 'n' roll to become a minister, and others like Carl Perkins, Fats Domino, and Bill Haley seemed to have lost the knack of making hit records.

Elvis Presley's continued success had a lot to do with his remarkable ability to change styles. The sixties would see him moving away from rock 'n' roll to pop, singing more ballads and mid-tempo songs. His image changed, he did not grow his sideburns for several years, he dropped the wild stage show, and his records lost the pounding rock beat. One of his biggest hits was "It's Now or Never," which was based on O Sole Mio, an Italian operetta piece! He recorded a whole album of religious songs, His Hand in Mine, with the Jordanaires, which revealed the influence of gospel groups like the Blackwoods.

He was well suited to pop, gospel, and rock material, and this set him apart from most other singers. As the Colonel said, "The wonder of Elvis is that he has the voice range to be any sort of singer that he wants to be."

In the beginning of April 1960, Elvis was back in Nashville for one of the most productive recording sessions of his life. From it came both "It's Now or Never" and "Are You Lonesome Tonight," which would sell nine and four million copies respectively. He also recorded most of the LP Elvis Is Back, one of his best.

Then came a new film, *G.I. Blues*, which featured him as a soldier and took place in Germany (though it was filmed, as usual, in Hollywood). Elvis explained, "It's not about my actual experiences in the army—they couldn't film that!" He was able to use some of the knowledge he'd acquired in the army when an M48 tank slipped its track during filming and he was able to do a quick repair job.

In July, Vernon married Dee, who'd been divorced from her previous husband. Elvis was supposed to be the best man, but he didn't go to the ceremony, because he was afraid that the press would spoil it. "Everywhere I go it becomes something like a circus, and I think a wedding should be a sacred thing," he explained.

Elvis bought the newlyweds a house just around the corner from Graceland. Friends would later say that he didn't want Vernon's new wife living in the house that he'd bought for his mother. Gladys was always on Elvis's mind. The pink Cadillac he'd bought her in 1955 was in the Graceland garage, and Elvis had ordered that it stay there and not be used.

But Elvis was kind toward Dee, saying, "She realizes she will never take the place of my mother—no one will, but she seems very nice. My dad was a good husband and never left my mother's side in twenty-six years. If he has found happiness again, I'm very happy for him."

A regular pattern of film and record releases began in 1960. There would be two or three films (carefully timed to coincide with the school holidays), and an average of three LPs and four singles. The other film in 1960 besides *G.I. Blues* was *Flaming Star*.

Elvis was an angry, half-breed Indian in *Flaming Star*, and it's one of his best films. It was produced by Don Siegel, who would later make his name with several films starring Clint Eastwood.

There were three concerts in 1961. The first two were charity shows in his hometown for a variety of worthy Memphis causes. Elvis was very generous to charities throughout his life, especially those involving children.

He helped the funding of St. Jude Children's Research Hospital, which was founded in Memphis by entertainer Danny Thomas. Children with serious diseases were treated at the hospital free of charge; and it gave Elvis considerable satisfaction to feel that he was able to help children, whose parents might be as poor as his once were, to receive the treatment they needed but couldn't afford.

The third concert was a very big affair in Hawaii. Again it was for a charitable cause, to pay for a navy war memorial. Elvis gave a spectacular show, performing longer than he ever would again, and included one moment when he "dropped to his knees and slid twenty feet to the front of the stage with the microphone in his hands, never missing a note." Ticket prices were as high as $100, and when some VIPs asked the Colonel for free seats, he gave them

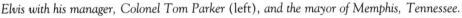

Elvis with his manager, Colonel Tom Parker (left), *and the mayor of Memphis, Tennessee.*

a firm no and explained that even he and Elvis had paid for a seat!

The Hawaii show proved that Elvis was still an out-standing live performer, yet astonishingly it was to be his last concert for seven years. He entered a phase of his career that would be dominated by filmmaking. He gave no live shows and made no TV appearances, and most of his records were film soundtracks.

RCA and the Colonel had developed Presley's career so successfully that it was now almost impossible to satisfy the demands of fans from around the world for visits and live shows. So they turned to the movies, which in the sixties provided the best way of reaching people in many different countries in the world, with a minimum of effort. A film could be made in under a month, hundreds of prints copied, and then sent out to be seen by millions around the globe. It seemed the best way of giving Elvis to his fans, and also the best way of making money. In 1965 Colonel Parker proudly announced that Elvis's seventeen films to date had grossed over $125 million.

The boom years were 1960, 1961, and 1962, with Presley records and films doing excellent business. Two movies, *Wild in the Country* and *Blue Hawaii*, came out in 1961. *Blue Hawaii*, made after Elvis's last concert, was particularly successful, and the soundtrack album outsold all his others—more than five million copies worldwide. Several singles made the top spot on charts around the world. British number 1s in these years included "Are You Lonesome Tonight," "Wooden Heart," "His Latest Flame," "Good Luck Charm," "She's Not You," and "Return to Sender."

But in 1963 his career began to go into a decline. He never lost his crown as "the King," he was still very popular, and he still made a vast amount of money; but his films became progressively worse, and the records lost the vitality and excitement that had made his earlier work so special.

Elvis was getting into a rut, and much of his work lacked sufficient care and attention, though it was certainly not all his fault. The system that had been devised by RCA to acquire songs for him, whereby the same people submitted material they thought would be suitable, meant that after a while there was no freshness to the new songs. They often sounded like ones he'd previously recorded.

The films were getting worse for much the same reason; the producers relied on story lines similar to the big successes like *Blue Hawaii* and *GI Blues*, rather than trying anything different. A typical Elvis film involved an exotic location, several beautiful women, and lots of songs. Elvis invariably played a happy-go-lucky young man in an unconventional job—trapeze artist, rodeo rider, frogman, pop star (many times), and was usually a nice, well-behaved person, but liable to have a fiery temper if he encountered a bully or a lout—so there'd always be a fistfight or two.

The films also got worse because the producers discovered that they could make them more cheaply, without apparently affecting the box office turnout. Lance LeGault, who worked on many of his films, told Elvis biographer Jerry Hopkins, "We shot *Kissin' Cousins* in seventeen days, and I think that film was the turning point in Presley films as far as shooting. Up until then certain standards were maintained. That's when we noticed there was no rehearsal for all the numbers."

At first Elvis defended his films: "I had a letter recently suggesting that I should get drunk or something in my movies, but the type I'm making now are doing so well that it would be silly to change the formula. I've done eleven films and they've all made money. A certain type

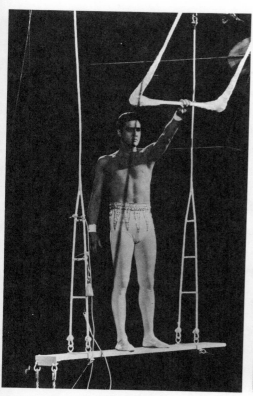

Top left: *Presley as Mike Windren, the trapeze artist in the movie* Fun in Acapulco. *Top right: In* Harum Scarum, *Elvis played a film and recording star who is kidnapped while on a tour of the Middle East. Bottom: Elvis had two roles in* Kissin' Cousins—*Josh Morgan, an air force officer, and the blond country boy, Jodie Tatum.*

of audience likes me and it would be foolish to tamper with that kind of success."

The eleventh film was *Girls! Girls! Girls!* in which Elvis goes fishing and then sings to the shrimp he's just caught! His soft image made a dramatic contrast to the more realistic, rough, tough hero of films like *Jailhouse Rock*.

After a while Elvis, too, was fed up with the film roles he was given. But he couldn't just stop, because contracts had been signed for several more movies to be made; and he wasn't able to choose which scripts were used. When his filmmaking days were over he would explain, "It was getting harder and harder singing to the camera all day long. Let's face it, when you have ten different songs for each movie, well, they can't all be good. Eventually I got tired of singing to turtles and guys I'd just beaten up!"

In the early sixties Priscilla Beaulieu moved to Graceland. Her parents were still in Germany, but they wanted her to complete her education in America. The Presley family agreed to look after her and arrange schooling (she was still a teenager), and she lived in the east wing at Graceland, with Elvis's aunt Delta Mae, and his grandmother Minnie Mae. Elvis did not see her as often as one might imagine, because he was frequently away making movies and staying at rented houses in Los Angeles, and when he was back in Memphis he spent a lot of time with his entourage of male friends.

The enthusiasm of his fans (which would continue throughout his twenty-two-year career) prevented him from leading a normal life, and so he virtually cut himself off from the real world. His involvement in films, shot in the "unreal" show business world of Hollywood, only added to his isolation from the way normal people carried on their lives.

He was increasingly living in a world of his own making, with his paid entourage who did everything they thought he would like. He was pampered, and everything was done to please him. When he showed an interest in karate, all his friends took it up; when he wanted to play football, they formed a team.

Like overgrown children they played at Graceland, with motorcycles, cars, guns, and adult toys of all kinds. There were parties that went on for days, all-night film sessions, hours of TV watching.

Elvis's Graceland lifestyle grew increasingly bizarre. He would sleep in the daytime, rise at 5 P.M. for a huge breakfast, then plan an evening's entertainment, perhaps a sporting activity or fun in a Memphis fairground hired for the night.

The entourage was always around. When Elvis was in Hollywood, they were there and involved in the filmmaking; when he was making film soundtracks, they were present. Over the years the number of friends in the entourage ranged from seven to twelve. They were all about his age, and each had a specific job. Some newspapers described them as the Memphis Mafia, and this term annoyed Elvis.

"I prefer to think of them as members of a little country club I run," he joked. "Most of them are my friends from back home. They are not bodyguards. One is my accountant, another my travel consultant. I need a valet, a security officer, and a wardrobe man with me nearly all the time."

Lamar Fike handled transportation, Gene Smith was responsible for Elvis's clothes, Red and his brother Sonny West handled security and were frequently used as stunt men in the films, Charlie Hodge helped with music and instruments, and Joe Esposito did much of the paperwork.

Elvis paid them $150 to $250 a week, which was not a particularly high salary bearing in mind how much he earned, but he gave them lavish presents from time to time, and most had been given cars.

The low point of Elvis's career in the mid-sixties coincided with the success of the Beatles, a four-piece group from England, who were the biggest sensation in pop music since Elvis's own emergence in the mid-fifties. Some papers suggested that they would take his place as "kings," but the Beatles themselves made it clear that there was only one "king" in their eyes, and that was Elvis.

As Beatle John Lennon explained, "Nothing really affected me until I heard Elvis. If there hadn't been an Elvis, there wouldn't have been the Beatles." Elvis was quoted as saying how much he liked them, and when they appeared on the Ed Sullivan show, he and the Colonel sent a good luck telegram, which was read out by Sullivan. He invited them to his home at Bel-Air, California, and they came on August 27, 1965. The meeting between the greatest singer and the greatest group in the world lasted four hours, from 10 P.M. to 2 A.M., and they chatted and swapped jokes.

7

The

Comeback

Elvis turned thirty-two in January 1967. Most of his entourage of friends imagined that he would always be a bachelor, because he seemed to love a carefree life, with several girlfriends. But though few realized it, Elvis had decided to marry Priscilla Beaulieu, now a grown woman of twenty-one.

As the year progressed there were signs that the couple were very close. They wore matching rings, and when Elvis's cousin Brenda Smith was in the hospital, she received a present and card that read, significantly, "Love, Elvis and Priscilla."

By April reporters had heard enough of these stories to be convinced that Elvis and Priscilla could marry at any moment. Their movements were noted carefully, and on April 30 they were tracked to the holiday resort of Palm Springs, California.

The same day close friends and business associates of

Elvis and the Colonel received mysterious telegrams in-structing them to go to Las Vegas. That night Elvis and Priscilla flew to the city in a private plane and visited the Clark County Courthouse, where they were given a $15 marriage license.

Las Vegas has unusual laws, and people can marry there very quickly and with a minimum of formality. There was no waiting period, as there would have been in Memphis, and that was probably the reason why they chose it—thus avoiding large crowds of fans and well-wishers.

At 9:41 on the morning of Monday, May 1, 1967, Elvis and Priscilla were married in a private room at the Aladdin Hotel by Judge David Zenoff. The groom wore a black coat and tuxedo trousers, the bridge a white chiffon dress with a six-foot train.

It was a short, eight-minute ceremony, and only four-teen people were present, including the Colonel, the couple's parents, and Joe Esposito and Marty Lacker (significantly the only members of Elvis's Memphis en-tourage to be present), who acted as joint best men.

After the wedding the couple moved into a large room for a wedding breakfast with a hundred guests, including several of the reporters (who were asked to leave their cameras outside until the end of the meal).

Afterward there was the inevitable press conference, when several reporters expressed their surprise that Elvis had known his wife since his days in the army. He looked nervous and said he felt more uncomfortable than when he'd first appeared on *The Ed Sullivan Show*.

"We decided to get married about six months ago," he revealed. "Priscilla was one of the few girls who was in-terested in me, for me alone. We never discussed marriage in Germany; we just met at her father's house, went to the movies, and did a lot of driving—that's all. I waited for her to grow up. We shall continue to live in Memphis, and we hope to spend a lot of time on my new horse farm in Mississippi."

After four days' honeymoon in a rented house in Palm Springs, the newlyweds went to the horse farm, the Circle G, Elvis called it, which was a few miles south of Memphis, just across the state border. They enjoyed riding horses and had a lot more room than at Graceland.

Back at Memphis there was a party for the friends who hadn't been invited to the Las Vegas reception. There was a coolness between Priscilla and some of Elvis's entourage. She didn't get on well with them, and most were about to leave the Presley payroll. Two were retained: Joe Esposito and Elvis's valet, Richard Davis.

In June, Elvis was back in Hollywood making his twenty-seventh film, *Speedway*, and Priscilla stayed at the rented house in Palm Springs. Then in September, Elvis was back in the Nashville recording studios.

The session produced some fine new recordings and marked the first indication of a return to the old form, a comeback from the sluggish days of the mid-sixties when so much of his music was bland and insipid—film songs with silly words and titles like "Do the Clam" and "The Fort Lauderdale Chamber of Commerce."

For the young fans of bands like the Beatles, Elvis Presley was a has-been. Their older brothers and sisters still regarded him as "the King," but that was largely on the basis of past achievements, and that enthusiasm was fading—the fan club membership had dropped, the films did less well at the box office, and the records scored low on the charts.

The songs recorded in September, including "Big Boss Man" and "Guitar Man," didn't sound like the work of a has-been, but of a singer who still had great talent.

They were released in 1968, the year that was to mark the turning point of Elvis's career. In January the Colonel announced that Presley would make a TV special for NBC. A month later there was more good news—Elvis was a father.

Nine months to the day since their wedding, on February 1, 1968, Priscilla gave birth to a baby girl at the Baptist Memorial Hospital in Memphis. She was named Lisa Marie, and thousands of cards and pink presents were delivered to Graceland from fans around the world.

Elvis was thrilled, explaining, "Oh, man, she's just great. I'm still a little shaky. She's a doll, she's great. I felt all along that she'd be a girl." The Colonel joked that he already had a contract ready for "the new Presley singer."

In March, Elvis was back in Hollywood, now living in a house he'd bought in an exclusive area of Los Angeles. High on a mountainside, it had huge, luxuriously decorated rooms and a magnificent view over the city to the sea. He was making the film *Live a Little, Love a Little*, one of his least known, and certainly best forgotten.

Meanwhile, plans were well under way for the TV special, which the Colonel had planned in an attempt to revive Elvis's flagging career. The director, Steve Binder, had very clear ideas of what he wanted to do with the show, and he had numerous disagreements with the Colonel. He was determined that it should be nothing like a typical "Elvis movie."

According to Binder, "I felt very strongly that the TV special was Elvis's moment of truth. If he did another MGM movie on the special, he would wipe out his career and he would only be known as a phenomenon who came along in the fifties, shook his hips, and had a great manager. But if he could do a special and prove he was still number one, then he could have a whole rejuvenation thing going."

Elvis and Priscilla Presley with their baby daughter, Lisa Marie.

The Colonel wanted Elvis to sing just Christmas songs (the show was due to be aired in early December), but Steve Binder wanted all kinds of songs, several from the early days, and he wanted Elvis to speak—to show the world something of what he was really like. Binder won because he managed to get Elvis to agree with his idea, and when the Colonel realized that had happened, he dropped his own ideas.

The special was recorded before an invited audience over four sessions at the end of June. Elvis was understandably nervous at the prospect of playing before a live audience for the first time in many years, and he couldn't sleep properly for several days before the recording.

All trace of nervousness seemed to have gone when he got on stage, though; he looked fighting fit and was in excellent voice. The show was a very lavish, expensive production, and some songs involved thirty dancers and just as many musicians.

But the highlight of the hour-long program came when Elvis, dressed in black leather, sat with musician friends like Scotty Moore and D. J. Fontana on a small, square stage, surrounded on four sides by enthusiastic fans. He joked and sang several of his best-known songs and gave one of the finest performances of his life.

The special, titled simply *Elvis,* was aired on December 3 and was easily the most popular show of the evening. It drew rave reviews. Critic Jon Landau wrote, "There is something magical about watching a man who has lost himself, find his way home. He sang with the kind of power people no longer expect from rock 'n' roll performers. And while most of the songs were ten or twelve years old, he performed them as freshly as though they were written yesterday."

One of the best new songs from the show was the pow-

Elvis performing during the historic NBC-TV special in 1968.

erful "If I Can Dream," which closed the program. Released as a single near the end of 1968, it was to be Elvis's first million-selling record in years.

The success of the TV special, coupled with a significant drop in income from films, convinced the Colonel that a change in Elvis's career was very necessary. He decided that now personal appearances would probably earn more money than films. Elvis's contracts with Hollywood companies stipulated three more films, but then changes could begin.

Elvis was obviously relieved, explaining, "You can't go on doing the same thing year after year. It's been a long time since I've done anything professionally except make movies and cut albums. Before too long I'm going to make some personal appearances. I miss the personal contact with audiences."

RCA intended for Elvis to make some more records in Nashville in mid-January 1969, but then plans were changed and he went into the American Studios in Memphis. It was the first time he'd made any records there since the Sun days, and the results were a dramatic improvement on almost everything he'd done over the preceding four or five years.

The producer was Chips Moman, who was having great success with records made in his studios which were scoring on the charts, by artists like the Box Tops, Dionne Warwick, Wilson Pickett, and Neil Diamond.

The reason for his success, according to Chips, was the superior Memphis session band he used on all the records. They were in top form for Elvis's two visits and can take a lot of credit for the success of the records that followed.

Elvis was in excellent voice, and the songs were far stronger than the film material he'd been churning out previously. In a ten-day session in January, and a further six days in February, Elvis recorded more than thirty songs, enough for two LPs and some singles, including "In the Ghetto," "Suspicious Minds," and "Kentucky Rain." It was a very productive recording session.

There were three more films. *Charro* featured Elvis as a bearded cowboy. "This is the first movie I've ever made without singing a song," said Elvis. "I play a gunfighter, and to be honest, we couldn't see a singing gunfighter." Next came *The Trouble with Girls* in which he sang only two songs, and then finally *Change of Habit*, an unlikely tale with Elvis as a doctor who falls in love with a nun. He would make only two more films, and both would be documentaries.

The Colonel had been organizing and publicizing a spectacular two-week engagement for Elvis at Las Vegas. He'd made a deal with the owner of the new International Hotel

A bearded Elvis in the movie Charro.

that Elvis would perform at the 2,000-seat theater there for $150,000 a week—an enormous sum of money.

Lavish stage costumes were made for Elvis, based on the karate suits that he found so comfortable, and an expensive collection of musicians was assembled. There was Elvis's band, which would be led by highly respected guitarist James Burton; two groups of singers to provide backup vocals, the all-female Sweet Inspirations, and the Imperials, a male quartet, plus a full orchestra.

Elvis was very nervous about the shows, perhaps remembering his first performances in Las Vegas back in 1956, which had been unsuccessful. He insisted on three dress rehearsals to make sure everything was right.

Elvis talks to newspaper, radio, and TV reporters about his upcoming shows in Las Vegas.

He shouldn't have worried; the teenagers who loved him back in the fifties were now in their early thirties, and for many Las Vegas was a favorite holiday destination. Elvis walked out on stage for the first show and the whole audience rose to their feet and gave him a deafening ovation.

The show was a great success, a mixture of old favorites and new hits. Best received of all was "Suspicious Minds," the new record which had given him his first number 1 since the early sixties.

A writer commented in *Newsweek* magazine, "There are several unbelievable things about Elvis, but the most incredible is his staying power in a world where meteoric careers fade like shooting stars."

Elvis performed for a month in Las Vegas, giving two shows a night, and was seen by 101,000 people. He was back at the top again; no one else could draw such crowds and earn so much money.

8

The

Las Vegas Years

The year 1969 had been an excellent one for Elvis, and as the seventies dawned, his future looked very bright indeed. He was riding high on the crest of a wave of critical and popular acclaim and seemed very happy in his private life, with a beautiful wife and young daughter.

In January 1970 he was back at the Las Vegas International Hotel for another month-long season. Some people suggested that it was far too early for him to return, just five months after his summer triumph, but the demand for tickets was as great as before, and there was no danger that Elvis would have to play to any empty seats.

The fans arrived in force from all over the country, and those who'd seen the earlier shows noticed a couple of significant changes. Although Elvis still sang many of his early hits and recent successes like "Suspicious Minds," there were several well-known songs that had previously been made famous by other people. The supply of new material from his regular team of writers seemed to be very low, so he'd begun choosing songs by other performers including Neil Diamond, Creedence Clearwater Revival, and Joe South. The audiences liked hearing Elvis sing these songs, and they became a regular part of his repertoire in the seventies.

Elvis's obsession with karate was introduced into the shows; he already wore a stage costume modeled on his karate suit, but now he began making karate movements during the songs, and later he gave between-song monologues about his hobby. Some observers were critical of these "demonstrations," but the fans were genuinely interested in anything and everything to do with their hero and were quite happy to hear talk as well as singing. To

Onstage in Las Vegas.

them, Elvis created a very special and a very personal atmosphere in the hotel's 2,000-seat theater.

He continued to use a large number of musicians for the Las Vegas shows: his own rock 'n' roll band; the orchestra; and two groups of singers, J. D. Sumner and the Stamps, who replaced the Imperials, and Kathy Westmoreland and some other female singers, who replaced the Sweet Inspirations. Elvis loved to sing and also to hear other voices, and as the Vegas session continued he gave them their own spot to sing gospel songs.

He was far and away the most popular performer in Las Vegas, a city dominated by big-name entertainment and gambling. The hotels loved having Elvis there because he brought increased business for everyone.

At the International, and at the Hilton (where he would perform regularly in later years), he didn't just fill the theater twice a night. His presence meant that all the hotel rooms were booked, the souvenir shops did a roaring business, and profits from the gambling tables and one-arm bandits increased dramatically. So pleased were the owners of the Hilton that after his fourth Las Vegas season they gave him a solid-gold belt, worth $10,000.

Two Las Vegas visits a year, in winter and in summer, became a regular fixture for Elvis in the seventies. For the rest of the year he gave concerts in other big cities, did some recording, and relaxed at Graceland.

His first big concert outside Las Vegas was in February 1970 at the enormous Houston Astrodome in Texas, which seated 45,000. The Colonel had figured out that even if the cheapest seats were only $1 each, he and Elvis would still make a great deal of money. Elvis was guaranteed $100,000, plus a percentage of the receipts, and after playing a series of shows at the Astrodome to a total of 200,000 people, he was paid a reported $1,200,000. But the concerts were not very successful from the point of view of the audience, because the acoustics were so poor. Future shows were planned for much smaller places.

Before the opening of the 1970 Las Vegas summer season, work began on a special documentary film entitled *Elvis—That's the Way It Is.* Directed by Denis Sanders, the movie followed Elvis through rehearsal as he prepared songs with the rhythm group, then the backup singers and the orchestra to the full-scale Las Vegas show.

That's the Way It Is marked the first movie where audiences had a chance to glimpse the real Elvis, a refreshing change from the bland film characters he portrayed in the sixties. Not much was revealed about his offstage character, but Elvis the performer came across as an extremely likable person, hardworking and very professional. Musically, it was a considerably more polished show than the TV special of 1968. Elvis was very pleased with the finished movie, saying it was the best he'd made in ten years.

It introduced his Las Vegas show to Elvis fans abroad and whetted their appetites to see him live in concert. As it seemed increasingly unlikely that the long-promised "world tour" would ever take place, many fans decided to go to America to see their hero, and as the Las Vegas shows were such regular events, visits weren't too difficult to organize. The summer season particularly became an international event, with large groups from England, Japan, and other countries where Elvis was "king."

The film was released at the same time that Elvis was on tour, and there was a big promotional push by RCA and the Colonel with record stores displaying a large number of his LPs.

While most of the Elvis records in the sixties had been film soundtracks, the majority of the seventies LPs would be live recordings or repackagings of older material. There

was an astonishing amount of repackaging—some very
worthy, like the "Legendary Performer" series which featured some of his finest recordings with previously un-
released items and extracts from interviews, plus handsome
booklets. Others were very poor collections, with a couple
of recent hits and some indifferent songs from the movie
days.

It was up to Elvis which new songs would be recorded
for LPs, but the Colonel was in charge of repackaging and
reissues. Despite the poor quality of some of these records,

*A special award for Elvis being presented by Todd Slaughter of the Official Elvis Presley
Fan Club of Great Britain.*

they all sold, because, as the Colonel had already discovered, there were many Elvis fans who'd buy every LP that came out, regardless of whether they already owned the recordings.

The early seventies were boom years for Elvis; his records were selling in large quantities, the highly popular Las Vegas appearances continued, and there were several record-breaking tours.

A film crew followed Elvis on one of his tours across America for another documentary, *Elvis on Tour*. The movie was released in 1972, the same year that Elvis gave his first concerts in New York City, at Madison Square Garden.

A nostalgia craze was sweeping America, and several acts from the fifties had come out of retirement to appear in concert once again; but the biggest attraction was still Elvis Presley. Everyone wanted to see him, and the audience for the four sold-out New York shows included many celebrities like ex-Beatles John Lennon and George Harrison, and David Bowie, one of the fastest-rising new stars of the seventies.

Two of the New York concerts were recorded for a live album that went on to sell more than a million copies. The Madison Square box office took $730,000 and Elvis received about a third of it.

Jerry Hopkins (one of Elvis's biographers) has estimated that with Elvis's share of the box office receipts, and income from the record, the star earned $1.2 million for just six hours of singing.

The following year he would do even better, earning $1 million for a two-hour concert in Hawaii. *Elvis: Aloha from Hawaii* was the most expensive entertainment special ever organized and was another brainchild of Colonel Parker's. It involved a concert Elvis gave at the 8,500-

seat Honolulu International Center which was beamed by satellite to TV stations around the world and was recorded by RCA for a double album.

It was a very lavish show: Elvis wore an expensive jewel-encrusted white jump suit, and there were several flashing neon signs that spelled out the words "We Love Elvis" in the language of every country receiving the show.

Aloha from Hawaii was seen by millions of viewers in many countries. It made its biggest impact in Japan, where an unbelievable 98 percent of the potential viewing audience was watching. The double LP was released very quickly by RCA and became yet another Elvis million seller.

As a performer it seemed as if Elvis could do no wrong, but in his private life things were coming apart. Priscilla left him, he had several bouts of depression, and he was having serious problems with his weight and suffered from ill health.

He was also being given a hard time by various newspapers. In 1973 the *Hollywood Reporter* said, "Since his return to live performing, Elvis has apparently lost interest. He's not just a little out of shape, not just a bit chubbier than usual; the living legend is fat and ludicrously aping his former self."

In 1971 outsiders first noticed that all was not well with Elvis. The critics who'd praised his 1969 Las Vegas shows began to criticize him, using words like "tired" and "boring" and pointing out that he was putting on weight, though all noted that none of the Elvis fans shared the critics' opinions.

Then came rumors that Priscilla was unhappy. Elvis's entourage of friends had been reemployed to help in Vegas and on the tours, and they returned to live at Graceland,

Top: *Elvis onstage during his special show from Hawaii.* Left: *A different view of Elvis, offstage, from the movie* Elvis—That's the Way It Is.

spending a lot of time with Elvis when he was relaxing.

This understandably upset Priscilla, who saw little enough of her husband because he was away so frequently, and then found she spent little time with him when he was home.

According to Jerry Hopkins, a normal day for Elvis in Memphis involved "going to bed at eight in the morning and getting up in the middle of the afternoon to have breakfast at five or six, then rent the Memphian Theatre for an evening of movies or on special occasions rent the Memphis fairgrounds." Priscilla didn't enjoy this kind of life, and when Elvis let Lisa Marie stay up all night she felt he was spoiling her.

According to Dee Presley, Priscilla became increasingly unhappy because "she was having to stay in so much. Elvis slept during the day when he was home, so they never got to go out." Priscilla also discovered that Elvis had other girlfriends when he was away from home.

A rift grew between them, and she started to do more with her own life, taking dancing lessons and, at Elvis's suggestion, learning about karate. Much as she loved her husband, she found life as Mrs. Elvis Presley too difficult, and she left him in 1972, taking her daughter with her to California.

Elvis filed for divorce in 1973, and after lengthy negotiations about money and the custody of Lisa Marie, it was granted in October 1973. The couple were photographed arm in arm afterward, and they seemed to be still the very best of friends. Priscilla was awarded a great deal of money, and Elvis was allowed to see his daughter whenever he wanted, though she lived with her mother.

His friends have subsequently revealed that Elvis was extremely upset when Priscilla left him, and that her departure was responsible for several periods of depression and ill health, but he put on a very brave face in public. When his wife and daughter were in the audience for a Las Vegas show, he introduced them from the stage and announced, "We are the best of friends and always have been. Our divorce came about, not because of another man, but because of circumstances involving my career. And nothing else! Regardless of what you have read or have been led to believe. I don't think it was fair on Priscilla, with me gone so often and traveling so much."

Since the beginning of the rift with Priscilla, Elvis had been suffering with health problems and they got worse after the divorce. Many of these problems were caused either by overeating or from the effects of drugs.

When Elvis was depressed he ate vast amounts of food, and the food he liked was bad for him. As Ed Parker, a karate instructor, wrote in the book *Inside Elvis:* "Without consciously realizing what he was doing, he would consume cheeseburgers, french fries, ice cream, Popsicles by the box, banana and peanut butter sandwiches, Pepsi-Cola, and a stomach-wrenching assortment of junk foods. It was as though he was trying to comfort the spirit within by stroking it with food."

Elvis's food binges made him fat very quickly. Then he would have to find ways of slimming down before a concert, because he didn't want the fans to see him overweight. The quickest way to lose weight was with diet pills. They added to the strain his body was already under from a variety of other pills—sleeping pills, painkillers, and "uppers" which he'd been taking in ever increasing numbers over the years.

He'd first taken drugs in the army and continued to take them when he returned to the United States because he thought they'd help him get more out of life. Insomnia had always been a problem; it seemed to run in his family, and he took pills to help him sleep, and then to help him wake up and to give him energy when he performed.

Drug-taking of this kind was quite common among young musicians, so Elvis was not unusual, certainly in the early days of his career. But his drug-taking increased at an alarming rate, and as his body became more used to the effects, he would have to take stronger doses to get the desired result.

Elvis knew that the drugs were dangerous, he read books on them and their effects, but he doesn't seem to have realized what damage they would do to him, and he never believed he was doing anything wrong.

According to several people who worked with Elvis during the seventies, he became very dependent on drugs and couldn't function without them. They did not have an adverse effect on his career until his final years, but they were certainly wearing his body down.

9

The

Last Years

Elvis celebrated his fortieth birthday in 1975. His career was now following a set pattern; there were two visits a year to Las Vegas and several short tours, taking in six or seven cities. These tours were frequent, and Elvis would be on the road for one week, then rest for three at Graceland before taking off for another week.

The touring must have been particularly hard on him because he was suffering from ill health. Sugar deficiency, intestinal blockage, pneumonia, gastric flu, eyestrain, obesity—all led to brief stays in the hospital in 1975, 1976, and 1977. The illnesses, largely brought on by his diet, his weight problems, and the effects of a variety of drugs, disrupted attempts to make new studio recordings but didn't cause the cancellation of many concerts, though some of his performances were affected.

The shows followed a familiar pattern, beginning with the dramatic theme music from the film *2001: A Space*

Odyssey introducing Elvis, who usually wore white, jewel-encrusted jump suits. Some shows recalled the old magic; others were full of errors with Elvis forgetting the words to songs he'd sung hundreds of times. Sometimes his between-song monologues went on for twenty minutes or more, and the musicians and backup singers had to concentrate hard not to look bored. He liked close contact with his audience, and he'd often shake hands with those at the front, blow kisses, and give away white scarves.

The fans continued to be very enthusiastic for whatever Elvis did, seemingly understanding when he gave a bad performance, but several journalists were becoming quite cruel in their criticism. Two articles that appeared at the time of his birthday were known to have upset him considerably and led to a lot of "hate mail" from fans to the writers.

The widely read *National Enquirer* printed a very unflattering photograph on the front page, taken at a time when Elvis was particularly overweight and looked ill. The headline read ELVIS AT 40—PAUNCHY, DEPRESSED, AND LIVING IN FEAR. Then the influential and respected music critic of the *Los Angeles Times*, Robert Hilburn, wrote, "Maybe it's time for Elvis to retire; at 40 his records are increasingly uneven, his choice of material sometimes ludicrous, and his concert performances often sloppy. Worst of all there is no purpose or personal vision in his music anymore."

But these harsh words didn't slow Elvis down; he continued to push himself into tours, performing far more frequently than any of the other big names in popular music like the Rolling Stones, the Eagles, and Bob Dylan.

Elvis gave no interviews in his last years, so it's difficult to know how he felt about these numerous tours and whether he thought about taking longer breaks or even contemplated retiring. But we do know of two strong reasons why he continued to work so hard. There was the insatiable demand for tickets from his millions of fans, and there was the very real need for a continuous influx of money. Though he was earning astronomical sums, his touring show was very expensive, and his extravagant lifestyle was eating away most of the profits.

The tours were organized to run like clockwork. Colonel Parker flew ahead to make sure everything ran smoothly, and an entire hotel floor was taken over and prepared for Elvis's arrival. The windows of his bedroom were covered in aluminum foil so that he could sleep during the daylight hours. Security was very tight so that no unauthorized people could get near him.

Hotel rooms are very similar, and so are the backstage areas of most theaters and concert halls. With the uni-

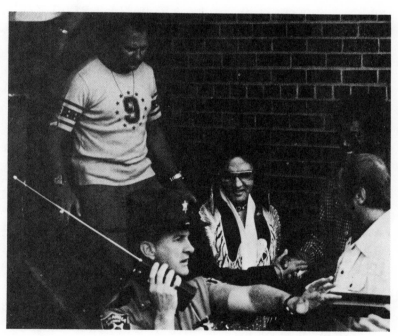

Elvis's arrivals and departures while on tour were well organized and tightly controlled.

formity of his surroundings and the blurring effects of the many drugs he was now regularly taking, it's possible that Elvis wouldn't have known which city he was in as he followed the almost identical routine of hotel–car–theater–car–plane–and on to the next hotel.

Traveling with Elvis were eighteen musicians, eight backup singers, six or seven members of his entourage (all with specific jobs), the sound and lighting men, the comedian who opened the show, truck drivers and roadies who shifted the equipment, and Colonel Tom's assistant. It was a very expensive operation, involving about fifty people, and Jerry Hopkins thinks it unlikely that Elvis would have gotten one out of every ten dollars he earned.

Large-scale concerts were arranged to try and raise more money. In January 1976 there was a show at the Pontiac Silver Dome in Michigan. The arena held 80,000 people, and the concert grossed over $800,000—a world record for one performance by a single artist. It was, however, a musical disaster. The sound was very poor; Elvis was separated from the backup singers, who weren't always sure what they should be doing; and the weather was so cold that the musicians had to wear coats.

There was quite a turnover among the musicians in Elvis's band. Several, who'd enjoyed working with him early in the seventies, left because they hated seeing the way his performance had deteriorated. Pianist Tony Brown has told a sad story of the concert when Elvis couldn't walk. "He fell out of the limousine to his knees. He walked onstage and he held on to the mike stand like it was a post. Everybody was scared."

Elvis was very ill, though it's uncertain how many people realized how serious his condition was. He managed to keep going on tours, but when he returned to Graceland he was frequently ill, often indulging in food binges that sent his weight rocketing up. Just three weeks after one tour, members of his band found him almost unrecognizable because he'd become so fat.

Dr. George Nichopoulos, who traveled with Elvis on many of his tours, has told Jerry Hopkins, "Elvis was a junk food junkie, and instead of helping him to break his bad eating habits, the cooks at Graceland prepared whatever he ordered. They had diet sheets in the kitchen, but it was hopeless. They mothered him to death. They couldn't believe they were doing him harm by making a fuss over him. He'd say "Fix a hamburger and fries," and they'd send up enough for six people." One of Elvis's entourage once joked that he probably held the world record for the number of cheeseburgers consumed at a single sitting.

Elvis spent several short periods at the Baptist Memorial Hospital in Memphis between tours. He would take several rooms at the hospital and his bedroom windows would be covered with aluminum foil. He was such an important

Baptist Memorial Hospital in Memphis, where Elvis was pronounced dead on August 16, 1977.

patient that his strange habits were allowed despite the hospital's normally strict rules and routine.

Though Elvis was supposed to be on a special diet, his friends would often smuggle in his favorite food. Back at Graceland he'd continue to eat the food that was bad for him and take the pills that it seemed he couldn't give up.

There seems to have been no one who could stop him on the self-destructive path he was taking. In 1976 a private detective friend named John O'Grady, Elvis's California-based lawyer, and Priscilla Presley tried to persuade Elvis to spend four months at a San Diego clinic that had a reputation for helping rich and famous people recover from serious drink and drug problems.

Elvis turned down their offer. He wouldn't even admit that he had a drug problem. When newspaper stories suggested as much, he would be very annoyed. He hated illegal drugs like marijuana, cocaine, and heroin, and he rarely smoked or drank. He convinced himself that the drugs he took were medication and therefore necessary.

He was earning more money than ever, the recent live recordings were doing well, and the "Legendary Performer" series and an imaginative repackaging of his Sun material were big sellers. The live concerts were breaking numerous box office records. But despite the huge sums coming in, Elvis was spending more money than ever too.

He'd had a reputation for being very generous with his money since the fifties, when he'd bought his parents a new house and his mother a pink Cadillac, but in the seventies his generosity seemed to get out of control. He bought the most lavish gifts for his friends and also for complete strangers.

One of the best-known stories of this remarkable generosity occurred one Sunday in July 1974, when he saw a woman admiring his Cadillac, which was parked on

Union Avenue in Memphis, in front of a car showroom.

"You can't have that, it's mine," he told the lady. "But never mind, I'll buy you another. Go into the showroom and pick the one you like." The astonished woman duly went inside and chose the car she wanted and was then given some money for new clothes.

On another occasion Elvis was in Denver, Colorado, and gave cars to two policemen who'd helped him out and to a doctor who'd treated him. A local television reporter finished a news bulletin with the story and said, "Elvis, if you're watching, I wouldn't mind a car too." It was a joke, but the next day a new car was delivered to the TV station, from Elvis.

An indication of the amount of money Elvis was earning and then spending came when his accountants had to reveal figures of his earnings for a court case. His 1974 income was revealed as more than $7 million, and after Colonel Tom had taken his cut, and wages and taxes had been paid, Elvis was left with about $1.5 million. Yet all this, and more, was spent on jewelry (Elvis had a friendly jeweler on call twenty-four hours a day), cars, and houses. Vernon tried to look after Elvis's business affairs and fre- quently tried to cut down his son's spending, but to little avail. Elvis loved to spend money, and much of it seems to have been spent on others.

It's said that in the last ten years of his life, Elvis gave away more than $1 million worth of cars to members of his entourage, to nurses at the Baptist Memorial Hospital, to all kinds of people who helped him, and to complete strangers who just happened to be in the right place at the right time.

He spent a lot of money on planes, buying a Corvair 880 for $1 million, then spending a further $750,000 on refurbishing it. This was used for his tours. He also bought a jet, which Colonel Parker used when making concert arrangements in advance. Then there was a plane for the musicians and another for Parker's private use, though he apparently returned the gift, perhaps knowing that Elvis couldn't afford to buy it. He knew that sometimes Elvis, the highest-paid entertainer in the world, was overdrawn at his bank.

Though Elvis was a very public figure, many of the most extraordinary stories about Presley and his spending, his drug taking, and his overeating didn't get into the newspapers. Until 1976 the members of Elvis's entourage were very tight-lipped about what went on behind the jagged stone walls at Graceland. But then Red and Sonny West, his friends and companions for twenty years, were fired by Vernon, presumably on Elvis's instructions.

They were given little notice, no explanation from Presley himself, and were very upset. It's thought that they were fired because their rough treatment of some overeager fans had given the Presley organization bad publicity.

Red and Sonny went to a journalist and told him they wanted to write a book. The result, *Elvis—What Happened,* painted an unpleasant picture of a man living in a bizarre private world of his own creation and increasingly dependent on "upper" and "downer" drugs.

Sonny said their motive had been to try and get Elvis to stop his self-destructive lifestyle. "He will read and he will get hopping mad at us because he will know that every word is the truth, but maybe, just maybe, it will do him some good."

The news that his former friends were writing such a book added to Elvis's depression and made it even harder for him to concentrate on the new recordings that RCA was desperate for him to make.

Since Elvis couldn't get in the right mood to go into the studios, either in Memphis or Nashville, the Colonel had the bright idea of bringing the musicians and equipment to Graceland.

There were two sessions, in February and October 1976. Much of the material produced was below standard, but the recordings did include "Moody Blue" and "Way Down," which were to be the last hits of Elvis's lifetime.

The only recordings made in 1977 were made at concerts. Most were recorded at shows in Omaha, Nebraska, and Rapid City, South Dakota, for his last TV appearance, a CBS special. Elvis looked far from well, was extremely overweight, and couldn't perform any of his characteristic karate movements. He sweated continuously and forgot the words to "Are You Lonesome Tonight." Yet despite everything, his voice sounded strong and vibrant.

He gave five more concerts. The last was at Indianapolis on June 26, 1977. Then he came home to Graceland, where he was looking forward to a visit from Lisa Marie.

On August 7 he rented a Memphis amusement park for the last time. With Lisa Marie, Ginger Alden (his new girlfriend), and about fifteen others, he rode the eleven rides at Libertyland.

August 15 was the last day of Lisa Marie's visit, because she was going back to her mother in California, and Elvis was due to start a new tour at Portland, Maine. Elvis spent several hours playing with Lisa, then after dark he went for a ride around Memphis in one of his cars. In the early hours of the next morning he played an energetic game of racquetball with Ginger and two other friends. He went to bed around daybreak.

At about 2:30 P.M. on the afternoon of Tuesday, August 16, 1977, Ginger discovered Elvis lying face down in the bathroom. He was unconscious. She quickly called Joe

Elvis Presley at his last concert, in Indianapolis.

Esposito and Dr. Nichopoulos, who were both in the house. They gave Elvis mouth-to-mouth resuscitation.

An ambulance was called and Elvis was rushed to the Baptist Memorial Hospital. A team of doctors spent twenty-five minutes trying to revive him in the hospital emergency room, but without success. At 3:30 he was pronounced dead by Dr. Nichopoulos, who said Elvis had apparently died of a heart attack. He was just forty-two years old.

An official Baptist Hospital statement described the probable cause of death as "cardiac arrhythmia and hardening of the arteries." A spokesman was quoted as saying, "Elvis had the arteries of an eighty-year-old man. His body was just worn out. His arteries and veins were terribly corroded."

10

The Legend Lives On

Elvis Presley's death was front-page news around the world. Just like his arrival on television screens in 1956, it was sudden and dramatic. There had been numerous stories about his health and physical deterioration, but even among his personal entourage of friends, there were few who realized that his condition was so serious.

There were unprecedented scenes in Memphis. Within hours of the news being broadcast on radio and television, a large crowd had gathered outside Graceland. Fans from all over the country began to arrive in the city. Most couldn't explain why they'd come—they just felt that they had to be there.

By the next morning there was a crowd of 75,000 outside on the highway, which had been renamed Elvis Presley Boulevard in the early seventies. There wasn't an empty hotel room available for miles. Thousands of fans had to stay up all night.

Elvis's body was taken from the hospital to a funeral parlor, where it was prepared for viewing in an open coffin, then driven to Graceland. Vernon Presley had announced that mourners could see Elvis's remains inside the house that afternoon, between 3 and 6:30 P.M., and 20,000 tearful fans walked past the coffin. Elvis's body was dressed in a white suit, a blue shirt, and a white tie.

The funeral was held the next day and there were 150 mourners. Priscilla, Lisa Marie, and Vernon Presley sat in the front row. Behind them were friends, relatives, and employees past and present. Actress Ann-Margret (who'd appeared with Elvis in the movie *Viva Las Vegas*) was among the mourners who'd flown from Hollywood. Colonel Parker sat at the back.

Some of Elvis's favorite gospel songs were sung by his favorite singers: Kathy Westmoreland, James Blackwood, and the Stamps. There were eulogies from comedian Jackie Kahane, TV evangelist Rex Humbard, and a local pastor named C. W. Bradley.

The pallbearers were Charlie Hodge, Joe Esposito, Lamar Fike, George Klein (who'd been a friend of Elvis's since they were in high school together), Felton Jarvis (who'd supervised the production of several of his records in the last ten years), and Dr. George Nichopoulos.

After the service a procession set off for the Forest Hill Cemetery, where Elvis was to be buried in a white stone mausoleum, near his mother. The white hearse carrying his body was followed by seventeen white Cadillacs carrying the mourners. The route was lined with Elvis fans. There was a short ceremony, then his body was buried.

The next day 50,000 fans visited the cemetery. Vernon was concerned about security, and when three men were arrested at the cemetery a few weeks later, apparently preparing to steal the body, he made arrangements that

the remains of both Elvis and Gladys be moved to Graceland, where they were laid to rest in an area now known
as the Meditation Garden.

Elvis's death caused a surge of interest in his life and
music. Within hours almost every record shop in the country
had sold out of his records. The RCA pressing plant began
to work twenty-four hours a day to meet the unprecedented demand.

Tributes poured in from all over the world. President
Jimmy Carter expressed his sadness and said Elvis's music
and personality "permanently changed the face of American popular culture."

There was a remarkable outpouring of books and magazine articles about Elvis, from many who'd known him
and several who'd had only the briefest association with

Vester Presley at his nephew's gravesite.

him. His uncle Vester, who'd looked after the comings and goings at the gates of Graceland, published his own slim volume of memories, which he sold to visitors to Memphis. A former secretary at the house, Becky Yancey, wrote one called *My Life with Elvis,* and a nurse at the Baptist Memorial Hospital came out with *I Called Him Babe—Elvis Presley's Nurse Remembers.*

There were many more, and all sold well. So did all kinds of Presley souvenirs, photographs, T-shirts, and records.

The Colonel, who came up with the slogan "Always Elvis" just a few days after the death, arranged that a close check be kept for people selling unauthorized Elvis souvenirs.

His hard work meant that he continued to earn money after Elvis's death. Lisa Marie was the main beneficiary in her father's will; Vernon was made responsible for administering the estate and then, on his death, responsibility was to pass to Priscilla until Lisa Marie reached the age of twenty-five.

After the funeral, investigations into Elvis's death continued. It was revealed that he had been prescribed more than 5,000 pills in the last seven months of his life, though it wasn't possible to tell how many Elvis had actually taken.

The exact cause of death was never properly established, but another statement from the Baptist Memorial Hospital said that it was probably caused by "polypharmacy," which means a combination of different drugs, a combination that caused a greater overall effect than would have occurred if they'd been taken individually.

Arguments about why Elvis died will probably continue for years, as will the speculation about the lifestyle he led.

Vernon Presley said, soon after the funeral, "Elvis was a good boy, he was generous as could be. He loved people and he liked to have a good time, just like everybody else. But the fans wouldn't leave him alone, so he built his own world and retreated into it. That's the saddest part."

But the fans aren't to blame for the lifestyle that Elvis led. He wanted their attention and was quite happy that Colonel Tom Parker, a hardheaded businessman, developed his career so successfully that he reached the maximum number of potential fans.

The saddest part of the story is that Elvis Presley's bizarre lifestyle wasn't necessary at all. As subsequent rock stars have proved, success doesn't mean you have to become a recluse, doesn't mean your life has to be spoiled. But all the big rock stars that followed Elvis had his experiences to learn from. Elvis, being the first, had to find everything out as he went along.

Any discussion of Elvis's lifestyle has to take into account his lack of experience. He had a double handicap: he was treading new ground as a rock star, and he'd had little experience of life before he shot to fame. Nothing in his early days could have prepared him for what was to follow.

As many writers have pointed out, Elvis never really got the chance to grow up. He went from being pampered as a child to being pampered as an adult. In a very short space of time he went from extreme poverty to great wealth. He was offered temptations that most of us will never experience. Whatever he wanted, he could have, including ludicrous amounts of fattening food and huge quantities of dangerous narcotics. And because he had such a superhuman talent, few people dared to challenge or criticize what he did in his private life. So he pursued a course that eventually destroyed him.

The only good thing that could possibly come out of his tragic early death is the influence it will have on others. Just as young musicians can learn from his music and great success, so they can learn from his mistakes.

Elvis Presley fans still flock to Memphis each year, with the largest numbers arriving in August for the anniversary of his death. They always head for Graceland. The mansion is now inside the city limits, because Memphis has expanded considerably since Elvis bought the building in 1957. The surrounding area was once farmland, but now it's built up. Directly across from the Graceland estate is a shopping center, with numerous souvenir shops cashing in on the Presley name, including the Elvis Presley Record Store, Elvis Presley Jewelry Shop, and Elvis Presley Museum.

Visitors are welcome to see the Meditation Garden and the ground floor of the house. To enter the grounds you pass through the iron gates, with their distinctive musical figures and notes, past the red-brick gatehouse, and up a winding drive to the house. The two-story building with imposing white pillars and two stone lions guarding the entrance has apparently changed little since Elvis's death.

There are now four gravestones in the Meditation Garden; for Elvis, Gladys, Vernon (who died in 1979), and Elvis's grandmother Minnie Mae Presley. There is also a small stone in memory of Jesse Garon, Elvis's twin brother.

An eternal flame burns at the foot of Presley's gravestone. It is mounted on a small plinth that bears the TCB and flash symbol, which was the slogan for Elvis and his entourage and means "Taking Care of Business." His fan clubs have changed the slogan to TCE, "Taking Care of Elvis."

A Gray Line bus tour takes visitors from Graceland

Elvis Presley Boulevard signs can no longer be seen in Memphis because fans have taken them all.

around Memphis. Driving down Elvis Presley Boulevard, the guide will explain that there are no road signs because they've all been taken by enthusiastic fans, and the city sees no point in replacing them because they'll be taken too!

Several Elvis landmarks remain in the downtown area: the Sun studio at 706 Union Avenue, which has been restored to something like the way it looked in 1954; the large Baptist Memorial Hospital, where Lisa Marie was born and Elvis and Vernon died; the B & H Hardware building, which once housed the Crown Electric Company, where Elvis worked; the decrepit-looking house on Poplar Avenue; Lauderdale Court; Humes School—now a junior high school; Loews Palace, now closed; and Beale Street, where Lansky's Men's Fashion Store still displays gaudy clothes in the window. Across the street from Lansky's is Elvis Presley Plaza, with a statue erected by the city in 1979 as a tribute to Memphis's best-known son.

In Tupelo, Elvis's birthplace has been restored. The surrounding area has been cleaned up, and there's now a

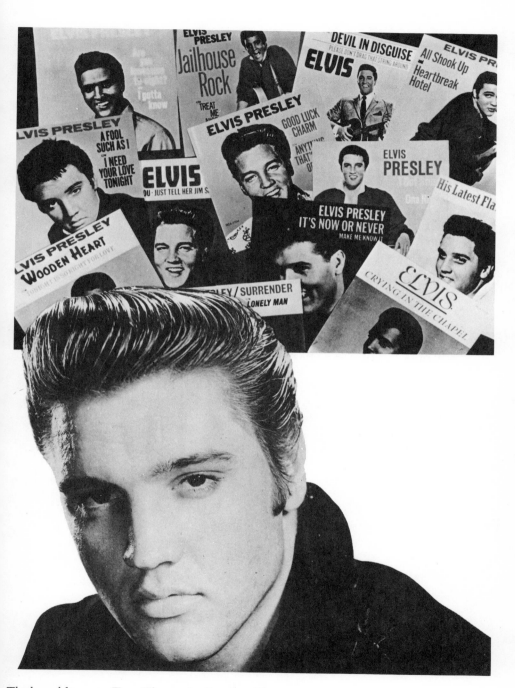

The legend lives on. Top: *The music.* Bottom: *The man.*

road where once there was a muddy track; but the inside is much as it was in the thirties—with cheap furniture and fittings. The difference between the numbing poverty of the shack and the opulence of Graceland is shocking; it's a whole world apart, and adds further emphasis to anything you may have read about the dramatic changes that Elvis experienced in his life.

Elvis Presley the man is dead, but there's a great deal left to remind us of him. We can still see him on film and, most important, hear his wonderful voice. Through records, tapes, and movies his legend lives on. Not only do his fans continue to remember him, but they are still introducing people to his music. Many who were teenagers in the fifties now have children who've become fans. For them, and millions around the world, Elvis Presley is still "the King of Rock 'n' Roll."

Acknowledgments
and Thanks

My thanks are due to several authors who have written about Elvis Presley's life and music. In particular I'm grateful to Jerry Hopkins for his two excellent books, *Elvis* and *Elvis: The Final Years*, which have been invaluable as sources of information. Several unattributed quotes have been taken from these two books.

Other books that have been extremely useful are *Elvis Presley* by Todd Slaughter, *Mystery Train* by Greil Marcus, *Lost Highway* by Peter Guralnick, *The Boy Who Dared to Rock: The Definitive Elvis* by Paul Lichter, and *The Sun Records Story* by Colin Escott and Martin Hawkins.

I've consulted magazine articles and newspaper reports in publications too numerous to mention, but special thanks are due to *Melody Maker* in London and *Rolling Stone* in New York.

Also of interest have been the following books: *Elvis in His Own Words*, edited by Mick Farren and Pearce

Marchbank; *Private Elvis* by Diego Cortez; *Elvis—The Films and Career of Elvis Presley* by Steven Zmijewsky and Boris Zmijewsky; *Elvis '56—In the Beginning* by Alfred Wertheimer; *Elvis We Love You Tender* by Dee Presley, Billy, Rick, and David Stanley, as told to Martin Torgoff; *Elvis Presley—An Illustrated Biography* by Rainer Wallraf and Heinz Plehn; *Elvis—What Happened* by Sonny West, Red West, and David Hebler as told to Steve Dunleavy; and *Elvis: Portrait of a Friend* by Marty Lacker, Patsy Lacker, and Leslie Smith.

Various people helped with photographs, and I'm particularly grateful for the assistance of Todd Slaughter, secretary of the Official Elvis Presley Fan Club of Great Britain. The photographs of Memphis are by kind courtesy of Jacques Delessert, Nyon, Switzerland. Very special thanks are due to Martin Hawkins, Gary Wallington and Bill Williams (WW Promotions), Lee Simmonds (at RCA Records in London), *Elvis Monthly*, Steve Frampton, and Lorraine Cobb. Thanks also to all the helpful and friendly Elvis fans that I've met in Britain, Europe, and the United States, and to everyone who assisted me during my stay in Memphis, Tennessee.

Richard Wootton

Index